Let's Go
ICE SKATING

OTHER SKATING BOOKS BY RICHARD ARNOLD:

Better Ice Skating (Kaye & Ward Ltd)

Better Roller Skating (first published by Kay & Ward Ltd)

Better Sport Skating (first published by Kay & Ward Ltd)

Dancing on Skates (David & Charles Ltd)

RICHARD ARNOLD

Let's Go
ICE SKATING

Photographs, line drawings, and covers by Richard Arnold

ELM PUBLICATIONS
King's Ripton
Cambs

British Library Cataloguing in Publication Data

Arnold, Richard
   Let's Go Ice Skating
   1. Skating
   2. Title

ISBN 0946 139 26 1

© Text, photographs and line illustrations: Richard Arnold 1987

© Cover design: Richard Arnold 1987

All Rights Reserved. No part of this publication may be reproduced, stored in a retrieval system, or transmitted, in any form or by any means, electronic, mechanical, photocopying, recording or otherwise, without the prior permission of the copyright owner.

Set in 10 on 11½ point Palatino by Fotographics (Bedford) Ltd and printed in Great Britain by Woolnough Bookbinding Ltd. Wellingborough, Northants, for Elm Publications, Seaton House, Kings Ripton, Cambridgeshire.

Contents

	Acknowledgements	vii
	Forewords	viii
	Introduction	xi
1.	Let's Go Ice Skating!	1
2.	The Great Adventure – First Steps	9
3.	Elements of Figure Skating	17
4.	Figure and Dance Skating	27
5.	The Basic Eights	35
6.	Turns	45
7.	Dance Skating (Simple Dances)	52
8.	More Advanced Dances	60
9.	Free Skating – Solo and Pairs	70
10.	Outdoor Ice Skating	92
11.	Now You Can Ice Skate…	94
12.	N.S.A. Elementary Tests in Ice Skating	99
	Appendix 1	110
	Appendix 2	130
	Glossary	135
	Index	147

TO TRUDY AND DAVID

Acknowledgements

I wish to express my thanks to the famous skaters who have been kind enough to write Forewords to this book. Unfortunately, there is no room to tabulate all their successes in World, International, and National events or the successes of their pupils. However, to my good skating friends Roy Lee and Anne Palmer (former World Professional Ice Dance Champions), to David Clements (former British Men's Figure Skating Champion, British Olympic Representative, and holder of many Ice Dance titles, and TV commentator on ice skating), to David Hickinbottom (former British Ice Dance Champion) I extend my gratitude, coupled with good wishes for their continued successes in the future.

Thanks to John Neal, formerly manager of the Westover Ice Rink in Bournemouth and home of former World Champions, now retired from the skating scene, for his kind words. John has been associated with the production of ice shows for the best part of half-a-century, and has made a magnificent contribution to this area of professional skating.

Thanks also to the National Skating Association of Great Britain for its co-operation in the provision of information and permission to incorporate into this volume rules and advice regarding its Elementary Tests in Ice Skating.

Offord D'Arcy
Cambridgeshire
England   RICHARD ('DICK') ARNOLD

Forewords

We are very pleased to be associated with this book by Dick Arnold. Quite often, after watching us training, or general public skating, Dick would say to us: 'Some day I'll write a book about this – for the beginners.' Well, Dick has done just that, and a good job he has made of it. As professional teachers of ice figure and dance skating we do appreciate the lack of something in writing dealing with the elements of skating. This book has been written simply, with the beginner in mind, and with its emphasis on acquisition of basic techniques and, above all, a good style, should be in every skater's library. We know Dick Arnold to have a lively approach to skating, and always to be eager to explore ways and means of helping the beginniner.

ANNE PALMER
ROY LEE

Anne Palmer and Roy Lee (Mr and Mrs Roy Lee) are professional instructors with a long list of successes by their pupils in Ice Figure, Pair and Dance Skating. They are former World Professional Champions in Ice Dancing and winners of the coveted 'Gerald Palmer Trophy' awarded in connection with World Professional Ice Skating Championships.

As a professional skating instructor, formerly a competition amateur, I have often felt that there is a need for a simple primer on ice skating. I am, therefore, very pleased to welcome Dick Arnold's contribution 'Let's Go Ice Skating' and delighted to have been invited to write a Foreword. Dick Arnold has been a skating friend of mine for some time and not only is he an enthusiastic skater but he is also a well-established author of many sporting books. This unique combination has resulted in a very valuable book to help the beginner to *understand* what ice skating is all about, as well as being of service to the enthusiast to better his or her performance on blades. Though conscious of the hard work involved in achieving proficiency in ice skating, Dick has never lost sight of its recreational value and its terrific 'fun' element.

DAVID CLEMENTS

David Clements, a former Chairman of the International Professional Skating Association and the British Ice Teachers Association, is a former British Amateur Men's Champion in Figure Skating, a British Figure Skating representative in World, European and Olympic Championships and Competitions, and a former British Junior Ice Dance Champion. Holder of the N.S.A. Gold Medal for Figure Skating, he has trained many pupils to success, and is also a commentator on radio and television for ice skating events.

When Dick Arnold asked me if I would be kind enough to write a foreword to his book, I was very pleased. Dick Arnold has been around skating, both ice and rollers, for a long time, and his enthusiasm and love for the sport are very apparent to all who meet him.

With this book Dick has broken new ground, as it is intended primarily for the beginner. It is a good primer which will equally be of use to the coach. The emphasis is on a happy approach to skating and a concentration on acquisition of the basic elements, without which no skater can proceed further; above all the author concentrates on the necessity of skating in good style.

I, too, share Dick's enthusiasm for skating and I would like to congratulate him on this book, and wish him, and his readers, every success.

D. M. HICKINBOTTOM

David Hickinbottom, twice British Amateur Ice Dance Champion and winner in 1964 with Janet Sawbridge of the coveted N.S.A. European Trophy, has represented Great Britain in World and European championships. He has been a professional coach and has successfully trained British Roller Dance champions.

For many years Dick Arnold has been known to me as a friend and as a most enthusiastic skater with a particular interest in Ice Dancing. A very neat footed style and a wide knowledge of techniques has developed with the long period that Dick has been a devotee to the art of skating.

I am happy to have been asked to write a Foreword because formerly Managing Director and producer of the Bournemouth Ice Follies I represented the reason for which nowadays many study skating in a serious way and spend hard hours at practice, 'show skating'. It is the aim to become a show skater that keeps so many skaters hard at work and perhaps I am more fortunate than many as I have been able to do something that I enjoy doing – a hobby as well as a career. Dick Arnold, with his clear and concise book will undoubtedly help many, probably setting some of his readers on the road to show skating, or to teaching the lovely and rewarding art, or to further improve and develop their ability.

JOHN L. NEAL
Managing Director and Producer
Westover Ice Rink, Bournemouth

John L. Neal commenced at the Westover Ice Rink in 1931, and was fortunate enough to be a colleague of the late Major H. G. Sharp. With Major Sharp and the late Phil Taylor, John L. Neal was involved in the presentation of the first Ice Shows. With the exception of the War Years (1939-45) when the rink was closed and John was away with the Navy, he has served continuously at Westover. During that period the show skating business has expanded and now has ramifications all over the world. John turned many leading amateur skaters into professionals, some of whom have become some of the most accomplished stars in the business, and 'discovered' names famous throughout the skating world. It should be noted, too, that Bournemouth has produced British and World Champions in Ice Skating as well as contributing to the professional show scene.

Introduction

Ice Skating is tremendous fun! You only have to *visit* a rink to see how much everyone is enjoying themselves – the atmosphere is full of laughter punctuated by an occasional shriek of excitement. No matter whether you are an absolute beginner or a more advanced skater, this sport exercises a peculiar fascination. Ice skating presents you with a challenge, it gives you a sense of achievement as each new step or movement is learned and it is, above all, a very democratic sport. Families, old and young alike enjoy skating together and helping each other.

Another of the attractions of ice skating is that you can indulge any enthusiasm you may feel for a particular style of music, classical or pop, by skating movements that *express* the music. Also, you can dance alone, either practising the set steps of the officially-recognized dances or doing free dancing, without feeling self-conscious. Imagine anyone dancing alone in a ballroom!

Ice skating is an international sport and it features in the Winter Olympic Games. Most countries have their own national ice skating associations which regulate the sport as far as amateurs are concerned: they organize proficiency tests, and arrange competitive events and championships. These associations cover all aspects of the sport, ranging from speed skating to dancing, from figure skating to ice hockey, and they have made very valuable contributions to the high standard of skating witnessed today.

The aim of this book is to show you how to get the maximum enjoyment from skating and to help you start skating correctly. You have to learn the basic edges, body positions, carriage and so forth correctly, otherwise all your efforts will be wasted at a later stage. Skating should be an apparently effortless, graceful yet athletic, flowing movement over the ice, and this can only be achieved by mastering the four edges (outside, inside, forwards and backwards) and getting the necessary soft knee action. All skating, whether figures or dancing, whether jumping or turning, is based on these egdes. Every skating movement requires a correct use of these edges; it is only too easy for a skater to throw himself or herself all over the rink, doing double or perhaps even triple jumps, spinning in many different ways, and look terrible! A less athletic skater, performing figures neatly and with style, with correct positioning of head and arms, perhaps travelling more slowly, though not performing the difficult movements of the first skater, will nevertheless not only look better but will also, in actual fact, be the better *skater*.

In the following pages I offer hints and tips that are the result of my own experience both as an amateur and as a professional coach. This book is not meant to supplant your instructor, but rather to help you understand what skating is all about, to help you supplement your coaching, and to help you to start skating properly before your first lesson.

A great deal of practice should be done *off* the rink, preferably in front of a mirror, so that you can see what you look like: to obtain the correct carriage, to check that your hands are carried naturally, and to see exactly what the position is that you are learning. By doing this you begin to know exactly how each position should *feel*. Each skating exercise should be supplemented by other physical exercises such as deep breathing, press-ups, etc. and smoking should be avoided.

Newcomers to skating who do not have an ice rink nearby generally skate for the first time on a frozen pond, where there are no rink barriers or bars to cling to. Because of this, they soon learn to get around by themselves. Whenever I teach a class of skaters, I absolutely forbid them to hold on to the barriers unless specifically instructed to do so (as in learning a Spread Eagle); I start my pupils from the T-position immediately, and on their second lesson they learn to stop and how to skate backwards. The T-position and other terms referred to in this introduction will be dealt with in detail in the following pages.

I hope that this book will enable you take the National Skating Association Proficiency Tests. The elementary Grade Tests for which badges are awarded are to be found in Chapter 12. These are official tests conducted by National Skating Association judges. Some rinks prefer to have their own tests for which successful candidates may purchase badges bearing the rink name. These are not official tests and have no value other than giving a rink publicity.

Now get your boots on and let's start skating!

1. Let's Go Ice Skating!

Once such an exciting suggestion is accepted, a whole new world opens up before you – a world in which you learn to glide over the surface of a rink with a peculiar sensation of freedom and exhilaration, almost like flying. It is also a world fraught with odd moments of fright, and the occasional bump and bruise.

THE ICE RINK

Some rinks are merely halls where skaters charge about the ice wildly, racing and playing, without any discipline whatever. These are dangerous places and have, in the past, given skating a bad name. Other rinks have special sessions for families, as well as dance skating and even speed skating. You would be wise to avoid the pop night rink sessions as these generally mean a disco with a disc jockey, loud music and lots of flashing lights. The 'teeny-boppers' who frequent these sessions are *not* skaters; such sessions do no good for skating, do not develop good ice skaters, and are merely a device to increase rink revenue by exploiting teenagers.

Try, therefore, to select an ice rink where skating competitions are held from time to time, where there is a professional coach or coaches in attendance, and where the music is suitable for skating to. Above all, try to go during a quiet session for your first venture. Winter school holidays and the periods immediately after the showing of skating championships on television often result in overcrowded rinks. As you will require room for your first ventures, try to avoid these times.

The rink is usually organized so that general skating goes round the ice rink in an anti-clockwise direction. No one is allowed to skate against this skating stream, because to do so would be dangerous. But, from time to time, an interval may be given to 'reverse' skating, in which the skaters travel round the rink in a clockwise direction. There may also be intervals for dancing, for fast skating, for ladies only, and for demonstrations. During these sessions you should only skate on the rink if you are capable of doing so without inconvenience to other skaters. For example, do not go on in a fast speed interval unless you are already competent to skate fast in safety, and are able to stop or swerve; do not go on in a dance interval unless you can perform the dance announced. Skating dances are set dances, rather like old-time or sequence dancing in the ballroom, and because skaters move swiftly it is essential that all the people participating skate the same steps, preferably at the same speed.

You can, however, learn a great deal by watching. Note how some skaters use their knees properly, how the expert carries his head, and how the dancers align their legs and feet. Observe what happens when a skater breaks the rules of good conduct by, perhaps, joining a dance sequence at the wrong moment or, inadvertently falling in the path of other skaters.

You are not allowed to smoke cigarettes or eat lollipops on the ice, as even a small piece of silver paper can lodge under a skate and bring the skater down with tremendous force. Dropping *anything* on to the rink surface is a very dangerous practice, particularly chewing-gum as it sticks to blades and causes accidents.

As you grow more confident, you may be tempted to skate faster and faster, until rebuked by a steward. Most rinks do not allow fast skating in the public sessions (except in specified intervals) because, with beginners and small children on the rink, unless a skater is in full control, there can be a nasty accident. Again, playing games like tag or tig and travelling together in chains or conga-files are banned on a well-run rink. Accidents, unfortunately, do happen to skaters and the practices I have described invariably result in someone getting hurt, usually not a participant.

CLOTHING

Everyone should avoid wearing headgear, long jewellery and baggy or very long jeans or trousers.

Until they become fairly proficient, girls would be well advised to wear trousers as they give some protection against grazes. A suitable blouse, jumper or jacket should also be worn. Slacks should not reach lower than the instep, otherwise they can get tangled either in the wearer's skates or in someones else's. After a few weeks, when a girl can move around with confidence, she may use more conventional skating attire: a small mini-skirt or a specially cut dress which flares out from the hipline. But 'way-out' colours and materials should not be used until the skater is really proficient, otherwise she will attract attention to herself *and* to her lack of skill. Under the skirt should be worn a matching pair of knickers or trunks, which can be sewn to the skirt, and these should be worn over the usual tights and briefs.

Loose jump suits or jogging outfits are ideal for the beginner and afford some protection against grazing in the event of a fall (*left*). More proficient girl skaters may wear a short skirted outfit or dress (*right*). Both girls are standing in the 'T-position' prior to making the first forward stroke.

Boys will find that slacks and a sweater or pullover are practical, though it is the fashon today to have special cat-suits or jump-suits made in stretch material. The beginner would be wiser, however, to leave these fashions to the very expert male skater.

In the early stages the beginner should not wear a wrist watch, firstly because it is easily damaged in a fall and secondly because pieces of broken glass left on the ice may cause injury to anyone who falls or puts a hand on them.

When skating in competitions, whether at rink, club or national level, and when skating proficiency tests, the candidate should wear suitable skating clothing: for the boys, slacks and a shirt or jumper, and for the girls a plain skating dress or leotard. However, some rinks do ban the wearing of leotards, while turning a blind eye to diminutive panties worn under a skating skirt – so please, girls, check first that leotards are acceptable to your rink management.

For outdoor skating you should not wear clothes that are too heavy, because you will warm up quite quickly, though a warm sweater should be kept handy to put on when you stop. Though the thought of wearing thick socks inside your boots may be appealing on a cold day, this is not in fact a wise thing to do: after the first few minutes skating, your feet become too tightly enclosed and your circulation is restricted, so that your feet get cold. Thin socks are adequate on even the coldest day.

If you get cold hands, especially skating outdoors, a pair of gloves is very useful. Do be careful though not to drop them on the ice for someone else to trip over. This can easily be avoided by sewing both of them on to a long piece of elastic or cord which goes up the inside of your sleeves and round the back of your neck.

HIRING ICE SKATES

Unless you have already skated on a frozen pond or lake in winter, you will make your debut at a rink, where skates are provided. Now, rink boots are not always very new! They have to withstand much punishment and ill-use, nevertheless they will enable you to skate without having to go to the expense of purchasing your own boots and blades. My advice is to use the rink equipment for several visits and not to buy your own until you know that you are going to take up the sport seriously. It is all too easy to become extremely enthusiastic and spend good money on equipment which, after a few weeks, you will not use any more.

It is customary to hand in your own boots or shoes in exchange for the hired ice skates. This does at least mean that you have the correct size to start with, though you may be a little dubious about wearing other people's footwear – especially footwear which had probably contained hundreds of different feet. So, the first precaution is taken before you go skating – make sure that your feet are well dusted with a good antiseptic foot powder, and that your stockings or socks are changed immediately after you have finished skating. Athlete's foot, an uncomfortable and itchy disease, is picked up very easily, particularly at swimming pools and from sharing boots. The simple precautions mentioned above help to resist it.

Do not wear thick socks or tights. The toes should not be tight and it is a good idea to specify skating boots about half a size less than your normal footwear. Rink boots are not easy to lace up properly, but you must be able to wiggle your toes inside them and they should be firm over the instep. Try tying a 'surgeon's knot' over the instep and then continue the lacing normally. Do not lace them too tight at the top as this will impede the circulation of your blood: it should be possible to insert two fingers into the top of the boot at the side.

BUYING BOOTS AND BLADES

These should not be purchased until you have decided that you are seriously going to take part in the sport. Fortunately for the skater who changes his or her mind, there is a ready market for second-hand boots and blades, especially amongst the children's sizes, but it is better to consider the matter carefully, as the outlay may be quite substantial.

When choosing boots, have them fitted at a shop which caters *specifically* for skaters. Most rinks have a skaters' shop which sells blades, boots, dresses, etc., and this should be the goal for the aspiring skate owner. The boots should be a snug fit and they should be bought *without* the blades fitted to them. The skating boot comes fairly high up

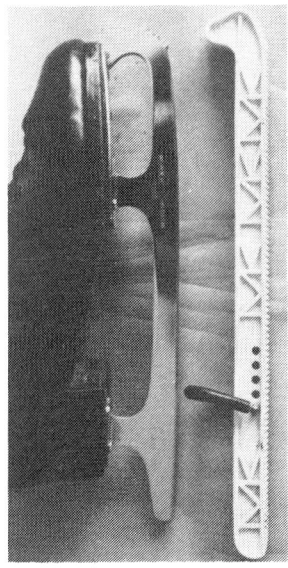 

(*Left*) Ice skate mounted on to boot. To the right of the skate is a typical skate guard, which is used to protect the edges of the blade when not on the ice.
(*Right*) Always make sure you remove the skate guard BEFORE stepping on to the ice otherwise you could have a very bad fall.

the calf and when the boot is loosely laced up, the heel should be held securely. The boots should fit tightly yet snugly, and allow for expansion of the leather, but, above everything else, the toe should not be tight. So, when purchasing, try on the boot wearing the socks or tights in which you are going to skate.

If you are a parent buying skates for a youngster, you will probably think, 'What an expense; he (or she) is going to grow out of them in no time'.

But children's boots do not get worn out by their first owner, they are outgrown. There is a ready market for them and many rinks have a notice-board which has 'for sale' and 'wanted' displayed on it.

Girl wear boots in white (or tan), whilst boys have black boots. When you buy boots and blades, you should also buy a pair of blade guards or protectors made of wood, leather, or plastic which fit over the blades to guard them from damage. Two warnings, however: (a) always wipe the blades dry after skating before putting on the guards; and (b) remember to remove the guards before stepping on to the ice!

Because there are no ice skating boots manufactured in Great Britain, they are imported from either USA or the Continent. It may be a little puzzling trying to sort out the right Continental size for yourself so the following chart should assist you. It commences with the smallest size and ends with the largest adult size.

English	Continental	English	Continental
10½	29	5	38
11	30	5½	39
11½	30	6	39
12	31	6½	40
12½	31	7	41
13	32	7½	42
1	33	8	42
1½	34	8½	43
2	35	9	43
2½	36	9½	44
3	36	10	45
3½	37	10½	45
4	37	11	46
4½	38		

CHOOSING YOUR SKATES

Once you have got past the beginner stage and are able to perform elementary curves, figures and dance steps, you will need to consider the type of skates you are going to require. If you wish to become an expert figure skater, you will need skates of an advanced design. Incidentally most rented skates at rinks are figure blades. If you aspire to becoming an ice dancer, you will need a special type of blade. By the way, skaters to do not talk about 'skates', they talk about 'blades'.

Naturally, the better the quality of the blade, the more expensive it is going to be, and you are advised to think carefully about the type of blade you are going to use and whether *you* will be good enough to do it justice.

Ice skates have developed into different types to meet different skating conditions. There are, of course, speed and hockey skates in addition to figure, free skating and dance blades.

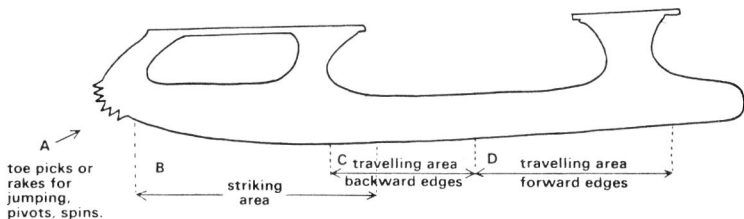

Analysis of an ice skate.

The part of the skate which is most important is the blade. Its thickness, contour and toe pick design determine the effectiveness of a skater's performance. Speed blades have a very long, thin blade which is nearly flat. Hockey blades have to have some of the characteristics of the speed skate, but are shorter and a little thicker and have a contoured blade, which gives more manoeuvrability than the speed skate or racing blade. Figure skaters need maximum manoeuvrability and the blade of a figure skate has a very short ice contact with about 7 ft radius. To help the skater jump and spin the figure blade needs toe picks; on the other hand racing and hockey blades are smoothly curved at the toe.

THE TEST OF A GOOD BLADE

The steel must be 'through hardened' to an almost unbreakable temper. This hardness ensures a high polish and retention of edge. The high polish is essential for a fast-running blade, whilst a hard edge reduces the need for re-grinding.

In order for the skater to have maximum manoeuvrability and control over his movements, the blade must be straight and its contour must have a perfect radius or combination radius, with freedom from 'flats', which would prevent clean turns and figures. Special attention should be given to the toe picks. Each skater will have individual requirements for this refinement. Let's consider the different types of blades.

Figure Blades

In order to perform high-quality compulsory figure tracings, the hollow grinding must be shallow. This is necessary if 'double tracking' is to be minimized. The toe picks at the front of the skate must be set a little higher so that clean ice tracing will not be spoiled by catching them.

Free Skating Blades

These blades require an extra deep hollow grind in order to prevent slipping. The toe picks are large, in combination form and include one large high pick giving the skater a really good ice grip when taking off in jumps.

Dance Blades

These differ in that the blade heel is specially shortened to prevent skates colliding during fast and intricate footwork. The skating edge has a reduced width to give fast smooth running, with a minimum of effort.

DO NOT be tempted to buy boots and skates which are on 'hire' at the rinks – a British skate manufacturer at the World's Ice Championships in Cincinatti in 1987 described his own firm's 'hire' skates as 'just junk, we stamp them out like sausages' – you have been warned!

2. The Great Adventure – First Steps

The most exciting moment in a skater's life is when he or she steps on to an ice rink for the first time. No matter how well you may have practised moving on skates *off* the rink, the moment you step on the ice all sort of things happen. First of all the skaters whom you have been watching and admiring suddenly become fiends, travelling at high speed and apparently bent upon your destruction! They appear from nowhere, cutting in and out ahead of you, while the other beginners become dangerous obstacles who fall in your path or, even worse, clutch at you in a frantic effort to maintain their rapidly diminishing balance. Secondly, you suddenly become aware that you have no control over your feet and legs. The rink surface has become a place upon which are absolutely helpless: you can go neither forwards nor backwards, you cannot start to move and, if you do, you cannot stop . . . ! Fortunately the problem of maintaining your balance gradually overcomes your apprehension about the other skaters, and the feeling of helplessness soon turns to one of exhilaration as you take your steps.

When you stand up for the first time, the ice skates will feel thin beneath you and there will be a tendency for your ankles to drop over, though you will be able to stand erect on the blades and move your ankles forwards or backwards. As you walk towards the ice, your confidence will return, but, a word of caution: you have to step *down* on to the ice on most rinks, through an opening in the barrier. The transition from walking on matting or rubber flooring to a slippery ice surface and stepping downwards at the same time is the most perilous moment in a skater's career!

Carefully stand with both feet together parallel to the barrier, and hold the barrier with your right hand. Keep all your weight evenly distributed over both feet. Make sure you are not going to step into the path of another skater, then carefully move your left foot sideways and place it firmly on to the ice. Stand erect and do not lean in any direction. Still holding on to the barrier, transfer your weight on to your left foot on the ice. Lift your right foot and put it down alongside the one on the ice and then transfer your weight so that it is evenly spread over both feet.

The floundering and wobbling, the thrashing of arms and perhaps even the falls which follow may seem interminable, but within a few minutes, you will be making your way round the rink. The first lap will seem to take hours, but each lap will become easier.

With confidence you have found from your first efforts on the rink, you are ready to start making your first skating 'stroke'.

T-POSITION AND SKATING STROKE

Stand upright and perfectly still. Your feet should be in a T-position, that is your left foot should be behind your right foot, with your right heel in the instep of your left foot at right angles. Your knees should be bent. Still standing stationary and erect, with your weight evenly distributed over both feet, gradually transfer your weight to your left leg. In order to push yourself forward into the stroke, it is necessary to anchor your pushing skate, in this instance the left one, against the ice. You do this by turning your left ankle inwards, so that the edge of the blade will give a firm base for you to thrust against. Now bend both knees *deeply*.

Keep your right foot directly under your body. Now straighten your left knee (rear leg) and transfer your weight to your right leg, keeping your right knee deeply bent.

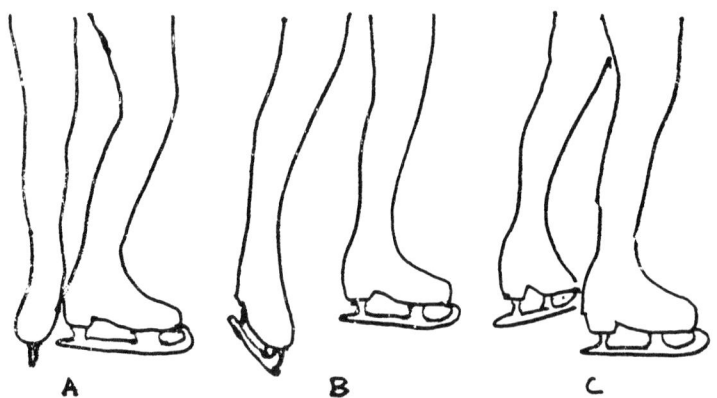

T-position and skating stroke
(A) Stand in T-position
(B) Transfer weight to front foot and push with rear foot: lift rear foot off ice
(C) Place the free foot on the ice and push off on to it.

Providing you have done this properly, your straightened left leg will start you moving over the ice on your right skate!

Leave your left leg behind, with the blade only an inch or so above the ice, and slowly bring your left arm forward to help you balance. Hold the glide forward as long as you can, with your body held perfectly upright.

You will thus have completed a skating stroke, and the next one to follow is done by bringing your left foot to the T-position against your right foot, heel to instep, and repeating the action: bend both knees, then straighten your right leg, which will propel you over the ice on your left skate.

Two strokes are enough to start with. Then stop and start again from standstill until you can *feel* the balance of each skate. When travelling forwards your weight should be to the rear of the skate blade and the push-off by the propelling foot must be done by using the flat of the whole skate blade. Do not use your toe rakes or toe picks to push off with.

Now try to travel a little further with each stroke, and you will soon be skating properly.

HOW TO STOP!

Having learned to move forward, the next thing to learn is how to stop. In most ice skating tests organized by national skating associations the first elementary tests are (a) to skate across the rink without falling down *and* (b) to stop when skating forward at a reasonable speed.

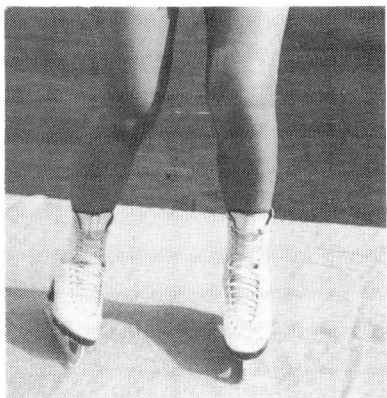 

(*Left*) Stop by letting the front skate curve round – the Snow Plough Stop.
(*Right*) In the Hockey Stop you swing the hip and both feet to one side.

Various directions may be given for stopping when skating forward, but they all have this in common: the use of the toe picks or rakes must be avoided.

When learning to stop, it is advisable to glide forward on both feet, with your weight evenly distributed between them. Keeping your feet about a foot apart, you should then turn your head to one side, generally to the left, and at the same time turn in the same direction on a sharp curve. As the curve commences, the foot which comes forward should then be turned even more sharply and your weight kept well back. The front skate will then bite against the ice with the side of the blade and bring you to a halt.

On the other hand it is possible to stop by swinging your hips sharply to one side, with both feet again parallel and about a foot apart, bringing your weight well back. Both skates will then slide over the ice to stop you.

Another method is to select the foot on which you are skating best, then allow the other foot to glide to the rear, about a foot behind the skating foot. Gently lower your free foot on to the ice and, by gradually increasing pressure on the blade, allow it to scrape across the ice and gently bring you to a standstill. This method does, however, require considerably more 'braking distance' than the other two methods described.

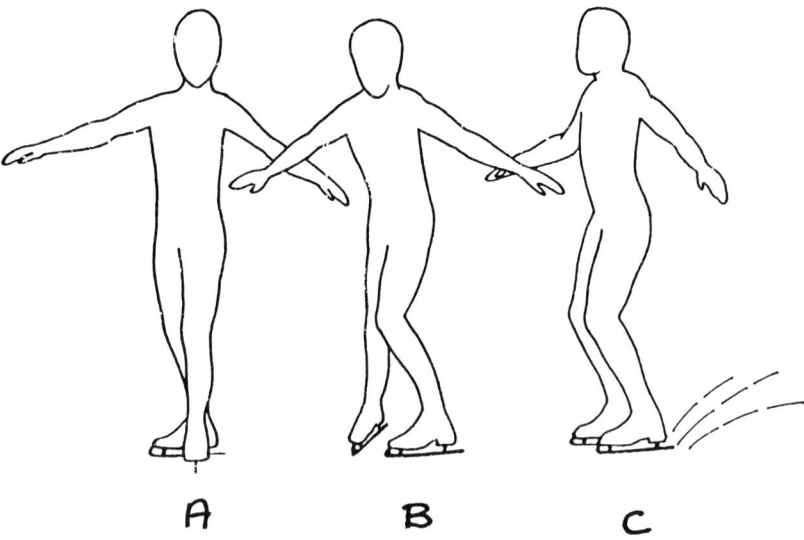

Stopping
A. 'T-Stop'   B. Snow Plough Stop   C. Hockey Stop

FALLING OVER

By this time you will have tumbled at least once – probably lots of times. When a fall is imminent, try to relax and allow yourself to collapse on to the ice. If you are tense or rigid, you are much more likely to injure or bruise yourself. Do not try to break a fall by putting a hand out; the ice can give you a 'burn', and it is possible to break a wrist by doing this. Also if your fingers are spread out on the ice, there is the possibility that someone will skate over your hand or fingers and cut you badly.

Let yourself go in a fall you have the time to realize that you cannot avoid it. Then, in order to get up again, do not try to climb up another skater or the barrier! Get into a position in which you are kneeling on one foot with the other foot squarely on the ice. Now, place all your weight on the skate on the ice, anchoring yourself by means of the toe pick if you wish, and gently raise yourself. The moment you are able to stand up, put your feet into the T-position so that you are ready to skate again. Do not try to crawl across the rink the reach the barrier, as this usually results in disaster!

CURVES AND RUNS

So far you have gone round the rink in a series of short glides and shuffles, but skating really consists of progression by means of a series of curves, not straight lines, and now is the time to consider what you are doing. If you look at your skates, you will notice that there is a hollow down the centre of the blade; this is termed *hollow grinding* or *hollow ground*. The two sharp sides of the hollow are called the *edges* of the skate. The edge of the skate on the inside of the foot, the same side as the big toe, is called the *inside* edge, while the edge of the skate on the outside of the foot, on same side as the little toe, is called the *outside* edge.

When skating curves, as we shall see presently, the skater does not skate on the entire surface of the blade, i.e. on both edges at once, but on one or other of the two edges. If you were to skate on both edges at once, you would not be skating an edge at all but on the *flat* of the skate. You must learn these terms now, as all skating is based on these edges.

Look again at your skates. The blades are not straight from toe to heel, but are set on a slight curve. This curve is called the *radius* of the skate – usually figure skates are on a seven foot radius. The use of the curved skate allows the skater to transfer his weight from forwards to backwards along the skate to suit the skating conditions; for example, skating forwards is done with the weight on the back portion of the

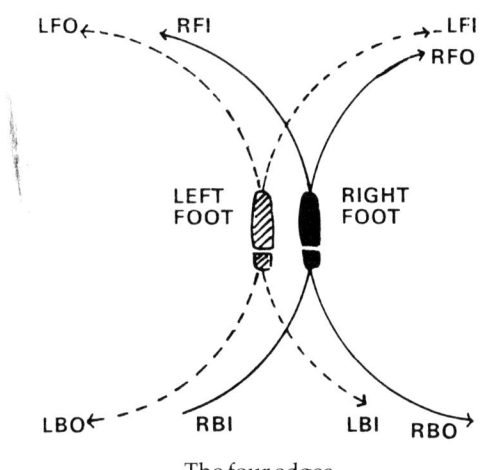

The four edges.

skate, and the front of the skate is clear of the ice. Certain turns are performed over different parts of the blade, and the toe picks are used for jumping, certain spins, and running steps.

A curve on one foot skating forward to the left may be either an outside forward edge skated on the left foot or an inside forward edge skated on the right foot. Likewise, identical curves backwards may be backward inside or backward outside edges. This may sound confusing, but in reality it is remarkably simple.

In figure, dance and pair skating there are only four edges – no more. These are inside and outside, forwards and backwards. Convention has decreed a certain identification code for these edges, which is used internationally. The capital letter R indicates a right-footed edge or figure; the capital letter L indicates a left-footed edge or figure. The smaller letter f indicates forwards, b indicates backwards, i indicates inside edge and o indicates outside edge. Thus: Rfo means an outside edge skated forwards on the right foot; Lbi means an inside back edge skated on the left foot. Certain turns – which we will learn about later – are identified by capital letters, but they do not concern us at this stage.

The whole foundation of figure, dance and pair skating is dependent upon these four basic edges. With the exception of certain movements and spins, all skating movements are a combination of these edges in one form or another and *a skater is only as good as the edges he skates*. For example, the take off and landing of even the most difficult jump must be executed from edge to edge (except in toe jumps) and special attention is paid by judges in tests and competitions as to whether or not a spring is made from a true edge to a clean landing on a true edge.

Thus, if you can realize that even the most advanced figure is a sequence of edges (requiring the appropriate body, arms, leg, head and foot positions), you are well on the way to becoming a proficient skater.

When you were learning to stop by coasting along on parallel skates and curving to one side, you were beginning to find control over direction skating, but you were not skating an edge, as you were running on the flat of the blades. Let us try, therefore, a simple curve on the outside edge of the skate.

Start by making a series of forward strokes from the T-position push-off. As you glide on you left foot, leaving your right foot behind you with the toe 2-3 inches above the ice, keep your left knee bent. Now lean to the left. At this point your body must be in an *unbroken* line from the crown of your head to your foot – no leaning from the waist or hips! You will feel the edge as your skate bites into the ice and you will start a curve to the left. Hold this as long as you can, then gently bring your right foot forward until it touches your left foot; bend both knees strongly and turn the toe of your right foot out to an angle of about 45°. Now straighten your left leg and, at the same time, step on to your right skate, and start leaning to the right. Then bring your left foot forward until it touches your right foot and go through the procedure again, this time stroking to the left.

You are now stroking and skating short curves or edges between each push-off or stroke. Try to lengthen each glide between strokes, counting 1-2-3-4, etc. as you glide on each foot.

CROSS-OVERS

As you skate round the rink, you will find that, whereas with your first short steps you were able to negotiate the curve at each end, it becomes increasingly difficult to get round with longer curves and strokes – the cross-over helps you overcome this problem. However, there is more to a cross-over than just using it to get round the end curve of a rink: it is a very attractive movement, especially for pair skaters.

Let us commence with a cross-over to the left, which is the easiest to learn, because it follows the natural progression round the rink in an anti-clockwise direction. Commence by skating on a left forward outside stroke, with your right foot extended behind. Now bring your right foot forward close to your left foot but, instead of stopping it beside your left foot, continue bringing it forward until it has passed your left foot. You are now leaning, with bent left knee, on to a left outside edge. Your right arm and shoulder should be forward, and your left arm and shoulder back. In other words, you are in a strong contra-body position, that is an exaggerated walking position. Now, cross your right foot wide over in front of your left skate into the inside of the curve. As your right foot is placed on the ice it should take up an inside edge and be absolutely parallel to your left foot. As you step over, your weight should be immediately transferred to your right skate. Your left skate will, virtually of its own accord, slide off the ice with the left leg in an extended position. Your left knee should be straight, and your left foot should be pointing, still in a crossed-under position, to the outside of the circle. Now, bring your left foot forward and stroke on to a normal left outside edge. You have thus completed the cross-over.

It is important that the skating knee should always be bent – it is impossible to execute a cross-over with straight legs. You must not push during the cross-over – the push is done on to the inside leg – the cross-over is a glide using the impetus of the original stroke. Remember that the knee of the leg which has been crossed should be absolutely straight and a smooth action must be striven for. Each cross-over means that you are skating alternatively an outside forward edge on the left foot and an inside forward edge on the right foot.

When you feel confident about cross-overs to the left, start circling to the right, i.e. in a reverse direction, and cross the left foot over the right, until you can do cross-overs each way smoothly, neatly and confidently.

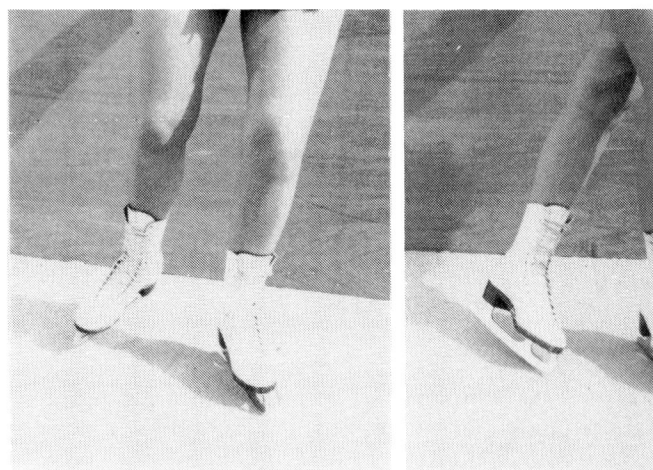

In the forward cross-over the free leg is brought forward and crossed over the skating foot, and when placed on the ice becomes the skating foot. Photograph shows a sequence: left forward outside edge – cross-over – right forward inside edge.

3. Elements of Figure Skating

Figure skating consists of solo skating by individual skaters and of skating in pairs (girl and boy), termed 'pair skating'. In professional and show skating, figure skating can be performed by a combination of several skaters, e.g. a trio, two people of the same sex, or by what are termed 'line' skaters in chorus or formations.

Amateur skating is controlled by the national ice skating associations of each country, affiliated to an international body, and figure skating is composed of what are called 'school' or 'compulsory' figures for solo skaters, plus what are termed 'compulsory programmes', that is a short programme with compulsory moves, for free skating and pair skating. Free skating consists of a programme of different skating movements – jumps, spins, edges and linking steps – skated in harmony with suitable music. In international and national competitions for amateurs, certain jumps and spins are specified to be included in the 'compulsory' short programmes for free skating and pair skating.

The skating must be carried out in accordance with basic rules of correct carriage, motion and flow. (There is a special style of skating, termed the English Style, which differs from the International Style in that compulsory figures, skating movements and turns are on a different schedule and there is not the same freedom of arm and leg movement; it is chiefly confined to a few enthusiasts in England.) The rules of style which follow are applicable to what is called the International Style of Figure Skating.

When learning basic figures, you must at all times strive to conform to the rules of good form, which are briefly:

1. There should be no stiffness of your body or limbs.
2. The upper part of your body should be erect and not bent forwards or to either side at the hips.
3. Your arms must not be held too high, and must be carried gracefully and easily to assist movement.
4. Your hands should not be carried above the waist. Indeed, one cannot stress this point often enough: stiff rigid fingers and

clenched fists are anathema; the hands should be carried with palms downwards and held naturally and easily.
5. Stiff, tense, or exaggerated postures have to be avoided. Thus, your skating leg should have a slightly bent knee and your free leg, which should also be slightly bent at the knee, should be carried over the tracing line.
6. The toe of your free foot should point downwards and outwards, and should be carried neither too high off the ice, nor too close to your skating foot.
7. Your head must be held in a relaxed and natural upright position.
8. You should raise and lower your body by bending the knee of your skating leg. Abrupt and jerky movements must be avoided, and the whole impression should be of a smooth, effortless flow, carried out at a reasonable speed.

FIGURE SKATING TERMS

In the above rules of good carriage for figure skating we have referred to 'tracing leg', 'free leg', etc., these are shown in the drawing.

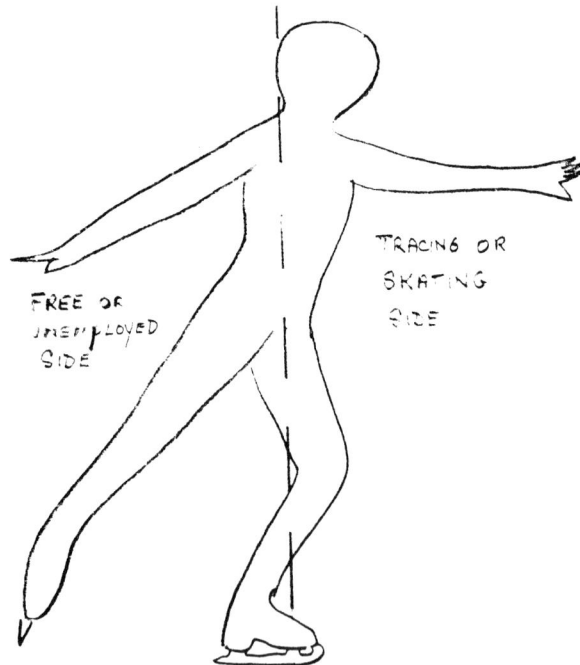

In this sketch the terms skating or tracing side and the free, or unemployed, side are defined.

FIGURE SKATING POSITIONS

With minor alterations to head position depending on whether you are going forwards or backwards, there are basically only four positions to be adopted when you are executing school figures (here we are referring to the edges and not to turns).

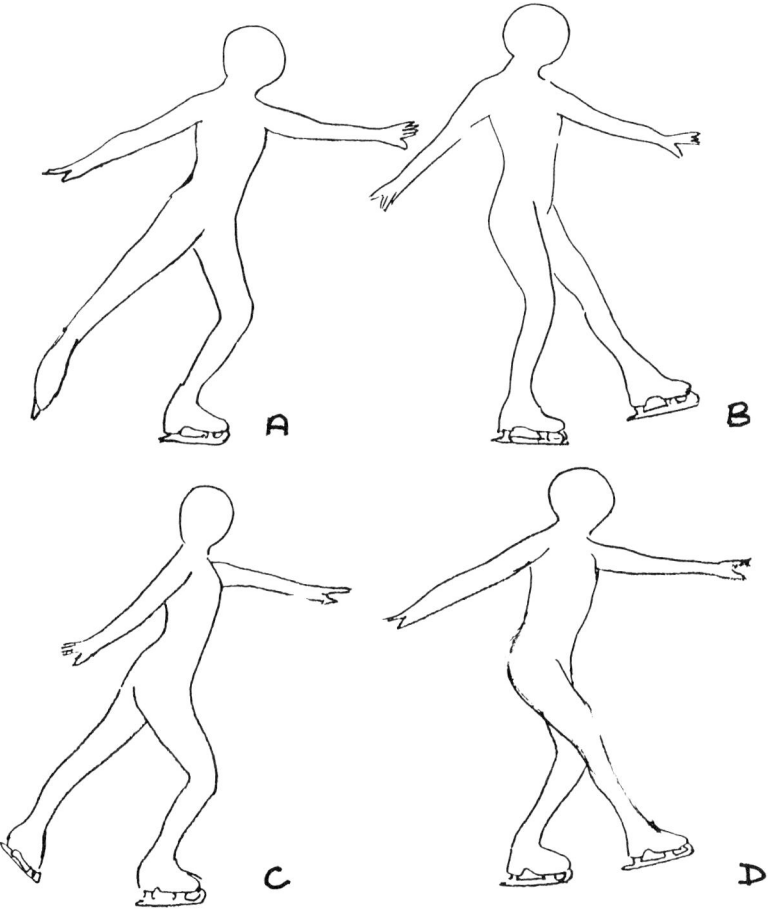

Body positions
A Tracing shoulder and arm leading: free leg, shoulder and hip back.
B Tracing shoulder and arm back: free leg, arm and hip forward.
C Tracing shoulder, arm and free leg back: free shoulder and arm forward.
D Tracing shoulder and arm forward: free leg and hip forward: free shoulder and arm back.

The head position will vary, because you have to look in the direction in which you are skating, but otherwise these are the basic positions. As you change from one position to another during the figure, there are of course intermediate positions to enable you to start the second half of the figure in the correct way.

SCHOOL OR COMPULSORY FIGURES

Apart from elementary and preliminary tests organized by the various national skating associations, school or 'compulsory' figures are skated over two or three circles, which join each other apart from a very small break in their continuity due to the skater changing from one skating foot to the other. The circles are all approximately of the same diameter.

The nomenclature of figures should be learned, for example, the circles (whether is two- or three-circle form) must be placed centrally over what are termed 'long' and 'transverse' (or 'short') axes (see diagrams). It is essential that you observe the placing of the figure so as to maintain both axes.

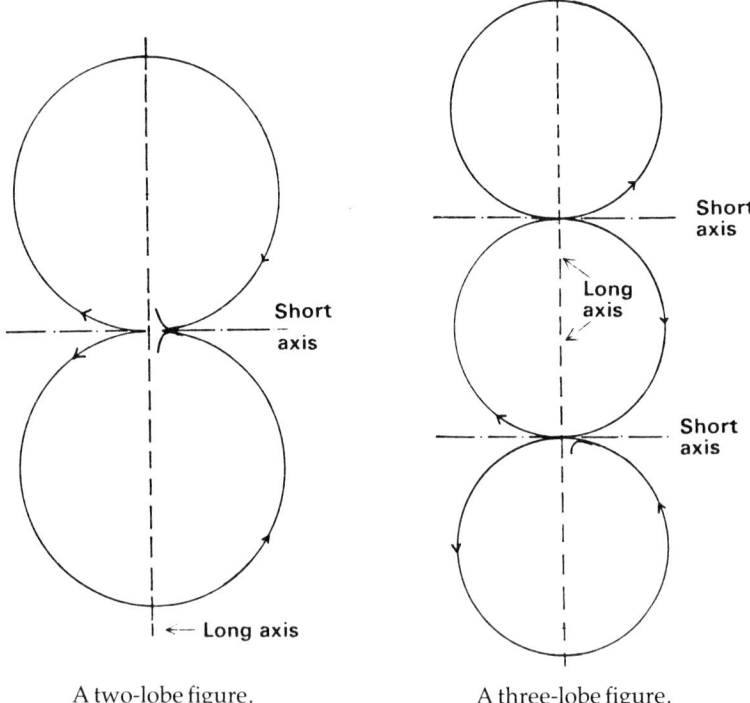

A two-lobe figure.   A three-lobe figure.

The skater has to indicate the long axis which he or she is going to use *before* the figure is skated. In competitions and championships the skater is not allowed to use the long axis provided by a figure previously skated, nor may he use ice markings (e.g. hockey or curling rings or lines) or mark the ice by scratching it with his skate in order to identify the start, the axes, or the placement of turns.

PRELIMINARY TESTS

Most associations which have elementary and preliminary proficiency tests do not require you to skate the figures over circles but allow you to lay down the figures on 'curves', 'rolls' or 'in field'. The strict rules applying to starting from rest, i.e. not employing preliminary steps to obtain impetus, do *not* apply to these tests. However, the standards insist that the 'curves' or 'rolls' should be sufficiently long to enable judges to see that the candidate has good carriage and deportment, can skate with reasonable speed, and has control over his or her edges. The lines skated must be free of wobbles.

Each figure which is started on one foot must commence in an identical body position on the other. This means a change of body position whilst skating the curves or complete circles, so that the current position is assumed for the take-off on completion of the finishing curve. At this stage, however, we will concentrate on the preliminary or elementary rolls or curves.

ROLLS OR CURVES

Outside forward: These rolls are skated first on one foot and then on the other, along the same long axis. Take up your usual T-position so that the toe of your right foot is along the line of the transverse axis. Your back will be to the centre of the circle you are going to skate. You will be sideways to the direction of travel, i.e. your skating shoulder and hip will be leading, while your free hip and shoulder will be directly behind. This is Position A. Turn your head over your skating shoulder. Keep this position when you have taken your stroke by pressing your free hip, leg and shoulder back, and leaning your whole body to the right. Keep your free foot turned out and pointed directly over the line made by your tracing foot. Your free shoulder must be approximately level with your skating shoulder or a fractional amount lower. *Keep your hips level.* You should feel yourself exerting a downward pressure on the free hip – this will maintain the correct skating position and correct weight distribution over your skate.

Inside forward: Commence with the T-position, but this time face your body squarely over your right foot. This figure uses a 'contra-body' position and the left or free shoulder and arm must be held forward, whilst you press the tracing or right shoulder and arm back. After you have made your stroke, keep your hips forward and your shoulders at right-angles to the line of your skating foot. Keep your shoulders level. Your free leg must be carried inside the circle or curve, quite close to your skating leg, with the heel of your free foot over the tracing line. Look over your free shoulder (the left shoulder) at the centre of the curve you are making.

The above two rolls or curves should be practised, stopping between rolls, until you feel completely at ease and happy about them. A certain amount of practice before a mirror is necessary to find out not only how the body and arm positions look but also how they *feel*, so that they can be assumed naturally and easily.

SKATING BACKWARDS

Oddly enough, most skaters find skating backwards easier than skating forwards! Skating backwards is not difficult to learn, probably because by the time a skater comes to learn to skate backwards he or she is already fairly proficient at skating forwards and has gained a sense of balance.

When skating forwards, you will have found that the feet are positioned so that the toes are turned out and the stroke is made by pushing with the whole of one skate from the heel of the other – the reverse applies to skating backwards. Logically enough, if your toes have to be turned out when skating forwards, then your heels have to be turned out when skating backwards.

Stand up, with your toes turned in towards each other and your knees bent. Now, transferring your weight on to one foot, lift the other completely off the rink and carry it backwards a few inches, placing it fair and square, with the toe still pointing inwards. This foot should only be carried back to about mid-way along the skating foot. So far so good. Now, transfer your weight to the skate just placed on the rink, lift the other foot, toe still turned in, and repeat the procedure. Keep standing erect, with your head up. You will find that you are able to walk backwards like this quite confidently.

After you have done this several times, as you lift one foot, press the skating foot (the one on the ice) and push against the other foot as it is

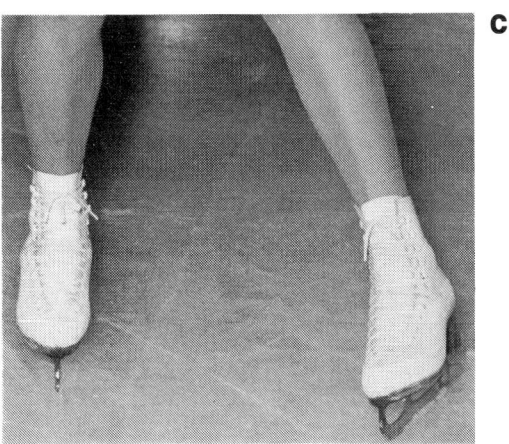

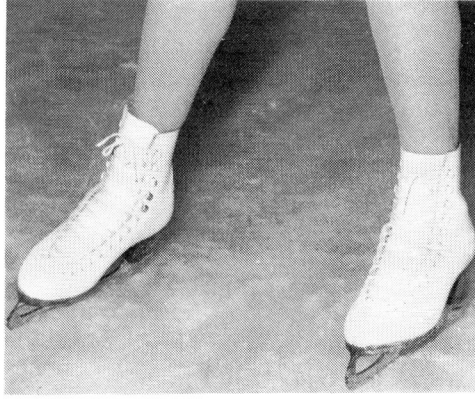

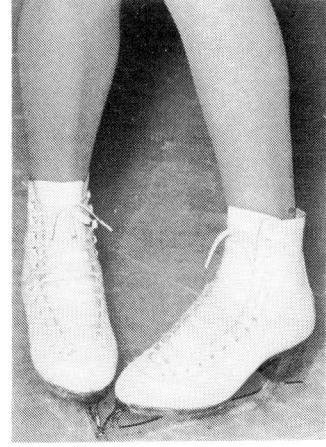

These three photographs show the backward skating sequence of strokes, commencing from the standing position with both toes turned in (an inverted T-position) (A), after the push-off stroking is from toe to with the free leg trailing (B) and (C).

placed in position. You will yourself skating on an inside edge backwards. Hold this position as long as you can, counting up to 3 between strokes.

Practise this for a while, then start again in the following manner.

Stand up perfectly erect, with knees bent, then (with toes turned in) transfer all your weight on to your right leg and at the same time slide your left skate off the rink surface in front of you. Point your left toe and straighten the knee of your left leg. This should bring your left off the rink and in line with the toe of your right skate. But do not lift your free foot too high! Now bring your left foot back until it is parallel with your right foot, but do not put it down on the rink just yet. Straighten your right knee and at the same time drop your free foot on to the surface directly beneath you and shift your weight on to it. Your right skate should lift off the rink in front of you and slightly to the right side. You will now be gliding back on your left foot, on the inside edge. Now lean your body on the next stroke to the side so that you will automatically stroke on the outside edge. The mechanics are simple: *you skate on the outside edge, but you push off from the inside edge.* Your weight must be transferred from one foot to the other when they are close together and immediately under the body. The free leg must be straight, while the glide is on a bent leg.

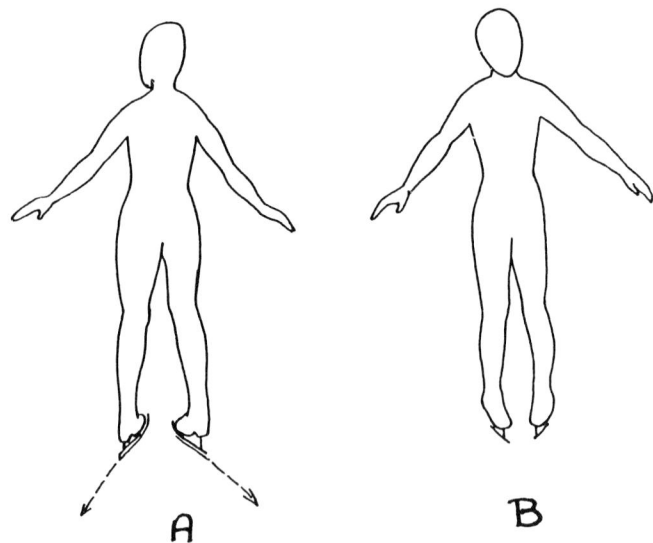

To commence backward skating turn the toes inward to obtain purchase to push-off. (A) View from behind skater. (B) Front view.

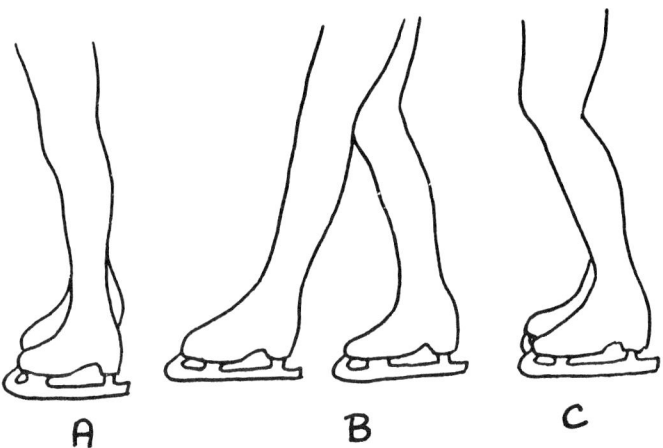

Backward skating stroke. A. Turned in feet. B. On one skate, free foot forward. C. Feet together for next stroke.
Direction of skating →

STOPPING BACKWARDS

When you are skating backwards and wish to stop, gradually bring your weight forwards so that your toe picks brake you. Alternatively, you can carry your free skate backwards as far as possible then place it on the ice at right-angles to your skating foot. The blade will anchor itself and, by keeping your weight forwards and gradually bringing your skating foot up to the anchored free foot, you will stop. Another method is to skate backwards, bring both skates parallel but apart, then swing your hips to one side and turn your skates sharply at the same time. This is the counterpart of forward stopping.

TURNS FROM FORWARDS TO BACKWARDS

Simple turns from forwards to backwards are made on both feet. Bring your feet parallel to each other, about 9 inches apart. Now gradually bring your shoulders round in the direction in which you wish to turn, e.g. if you wish to turn to the left, in an anti-clockwise direction, pull your left shoulder back and bring your right shoulder and arm forwards. Now quickly shift your weight from the back part of the blades to the part of the blades which is just forward of centre. Bring your right hip forward under your right shoulder and you will automatically turn on both skates at once into a backwards position. Do not lean forwards at all, but maintain an erect position. Keep your body at right angles to the skates when you have turned backwards.

4. Figure and Dance Skating

Most beginners imagine, quite wrongly, that free skating and dance skating are for experts only. They are under the impression, again quite wrongly, that one is virtually compelled to skate for proficiency tests. This impression is probably gained because most dancing on skates is limited to the schedule of dances approved by the National Association, and may be either the subject of tests or be used as compulsory dances in international competitions and championships.

This situation is often very discouraging to the keen skater. He or she probably wishes to be able to turn from backwards to forwards and vice versa, to skate simple dance steps, and to be able to skate solo to music (free skating) without wishing to pass any national proficiency tests. In other words, there are today untold thousands of skaters who could improve their standards and participate in *social* skating, including dancing, if more imagination were used by including simple non-official dances in public skating sessions.

We hope that the notes which follow will enable the average enthusiast to skate safely and enjoy certain basic dances, and, in a later chapter, you will be introduced to dances which do not appear in the international schedule, but which nevertheless *required skating skill* and are very enjoyable to perform.

OPEN CHASSÉ

In this step you put your free foot on to the rink alongside your skating foot and, as both feet are momentarily together on the ice, the original skating foot is lifted, the free foot becomes the skating foot for a moment, then the original skating foot is replaced alongside and the original skating position is assumed.

This may sound complicated, so try this in practice first without skates. Stand on both feet. Step forward (without stroking) on to your left foot – this would mean, if you were on skates, that your left foot would be the skating foot. Hold your right leg and foot behind as if you

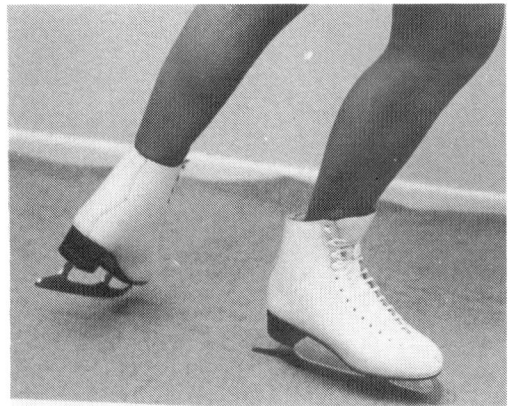

The forward chassé sequence (direction of skating →)

had just taken a stroke. Now bring your right foot forward parallel to your left foot. Place it on the ground. Do not pass your left foot with your right foot. Lift your left foot clear of the floor, not too high, and stand on your right foot for a second. Then quickly replace your left foot alongside your right foot, and lift your right leg back in the free leg position of a stroke.

The chasssé has thus been completed to the left. Now bring your right foot forward into the T-position and strike from the left to right foot, and repeat the chassé movement, this time to the right.

Now you can practise this with your skates on, but remember: as one

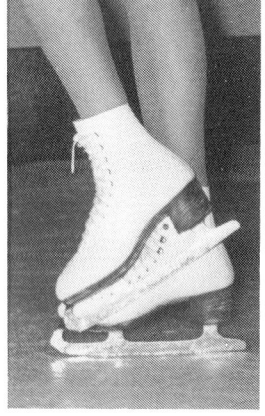

The backward chassé sequence (direction of skating →)

foot goes down beside the other, the original skating foot is lifted and then replaced.

A good free leg and a good bent skating knee are essential if a chassé is to be performed properly. One sometimes see skaters bringing their free leg alongside their skating foot and then pushing forward on to the skating foot – this is *not* a chassé. Incidentally, it is a very bad habit to lift only the rear of the skate instead of the whole of it, and there is often a tendency to lift the foot too high. The skate should merely be lifted enough to ensure that it is clear of the ice.

You should practise this chassé both forwards and backwards – the movements are the same in either direction and are easy to learn.

CROSSED CHASSÉ

This is a little more difficult, but, providing you have mastered your edges and forward cross-overs, a crossed chassé is fairly quickly learned. Practise a forward crossed chassé without skates first of all.

Stand on your left foot in a skating position, with your right foot and leg stretched behind in a free position. Now, keeping your weight over your left foot, bring your right foot behind your left foot so that your feet are in a crossed position. Lift your left foot from in front of your right foot so that your right foot becomes the skating foot. Practise this repeatedly from foot to foot.

There is a difference, however, when you are skating a crossed chassé backwards. When skating forwards the free foot is crossed behind the

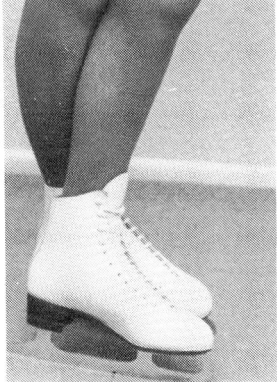

This shows the cross behind chassé in which the free foot is crossed behind on the outside of the skating foot (direction of skating →).

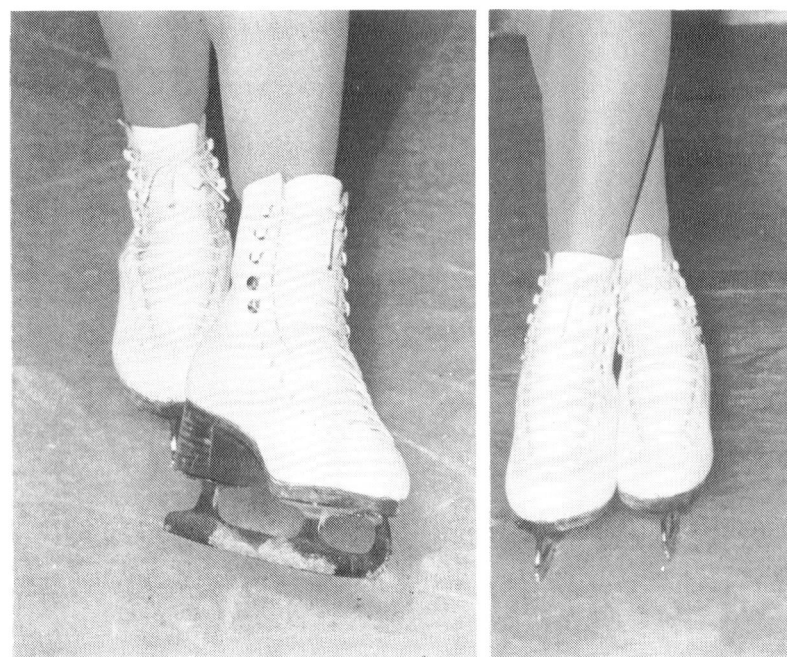

Front view of forward crossed chassé and trailing view of backward crossed chassé.

skating foot, whereas when skating backwards the free foot is crossed in front, i.e. the calf of the free leg is placed across the shin of the skating leg. So this time, for 'dry' practice, stand on your right foot with your left foot extended forwards; draw your left foot back across the front of your skating foot, place it on the ground, transfer your weight on to your left foot and then return to your original position. Repeat this in both directions until the movements are second-nature to you, then put on your skates and try it out on the rink.

PROGRESSIVES

Frequently also called a 'run', this terms refers to a movement in which the free foot passes the skating foot and is then placed on the rink, with the original skating foot becoming the free foot trailing behind. Without skates on the movements are: starting on your left foot skating, bring your right foot forwards past the skating foot and, as you step on to your right foot, lift your left foot and let it assume a 'free' foot position behind your right foot.

BACKWARD CROSS-OVERS

As might be expected, backward cross-overs are the reverse of the forward movements, but there must be a constant lean into the circle. Let us take the cross-over going in the general direction of rink skating, i.e. in an anti-clockwise direction. Remember that the inside shoulder and arm must be pressed back, whilst the outside shoulder and arm should be a little higher and held in front of you. The photographs explain what to do. Push on the right outside edge backwards and glide on the cross-over.

Backward cross-over sequence in which the right back outside edge is replaced by an inside edge skated backwards on the left foot, which is crossed over in front of the shin of the right foot (direction of skating ↶).

SKATING TO MUSIC

So far we have progressed by learning the skating strokes, curves and simple chassés, but the real beauty of skating lies in skating your edges and turns, or whatever, to music. At first this will be merely skating forward and stroking in time to the music; later you will learn the dance steps and how to keep time to the appropriate rhythm. This may be accompanied by a strong desire to free skate, using your own steps and edges, to music of your own choice.

One hears about skaters 'interpreting' music; this is not strictly so, unless they are skating in a show. A skater expresses his reaction to the music. It is easy to refer to musical interpretation but it would be more accurate to talk about 'musical expression'. Choose music, whether it be pop or classical, that inspires you to skate and create your own programme.

If you are going to dance on skates, you will find a great difference from ballroom dancing. Whereas dance steps are taken on the rhythmic beat (except for certain poses in modern Latin American and ballroom dancing), as a skater you will find that you may have to hold an edge or change of edge for several beats! Again, whereas in ballroom dancing one learns steps and then puts them together in a sequence, in skate dancing the free dancing is limited to the higher proficiency tests, competitions and championships. Modern ice dancing is more like modern sequence and Old Tyme dancing in that the steps are approved in a certain sequence, and the patterns have to conform (in the majority of dances) to a certain design on the rink. There are, in effect, three types of set dance: (a) the set pattern in which certain steps always take place at specifically identified places on the rink; (b) the preferred pattern dance in which different patterns may be used, but in which the dancers must maintain the repetition; (c) a border dance, which is progressive around the rink.

First of all, it is necessary to learn to stroke and hold edges to the different rhythms and tempi. Suppose we commence with the waltz tempo. It is best to begin with waltz music at 3/4 at 45 bars per minute. This is the tempo for the European Waltz, though other waltzes have the music and tempi approved at 3/4 at 58 bars per minute (e.g. Starlight Waltz), 3/4 at 66 bars per minute (American Waltz), and 3/4 at 54 bars per minute (Westminster Waltz).

Assume your customary T-position for the start and wait for the music to begin. Do not start your first stroke until there is a *strong* beat on which to commence. Listen to the music carefully and count the time as you skate from edge to edge 1-2-3 (Lfo 1-2-3, Rfo 1-2-3), etc.

When you feel that you are keeping in time to the music, you should also feel a good rise and fall of the skating knee so that you develop a soft knee action. All jerkiness must disappear: your skating must be smooth and in time to the music from edge to edge and from stroke to stroke. When skating to music, all steps must be made from heel to heel, and shoulders and hips must be held in parallel position.

As the music helps you with the rise and fall and striking, you will also find that you will acquire stronger edges, i.e. the curvature will be greater. *Do not progress in a straight line when skating to music.*

Having skated forwards to waltz time, turn and skate your edges backwards to the same music, remembering of course to keep a watch to the rear so that you do not collide with another skater or even the barrier! It is impossible to keep time, if your stroking is wrong. The main difficulty in keeping time for many skaters seems to be that they are ahead of the music, i.e. they skate out of time by being too fast. Rarely, if ever, is a skater behind the music. The golden rule is: hold back until you feel that it is almost too late and then execute the movement – 100/1 you will then be in time – this is particularly so where turns have to be made, as there is a tendency to turn too early.

In free skating, as opposed to dancing, the skater does not have to

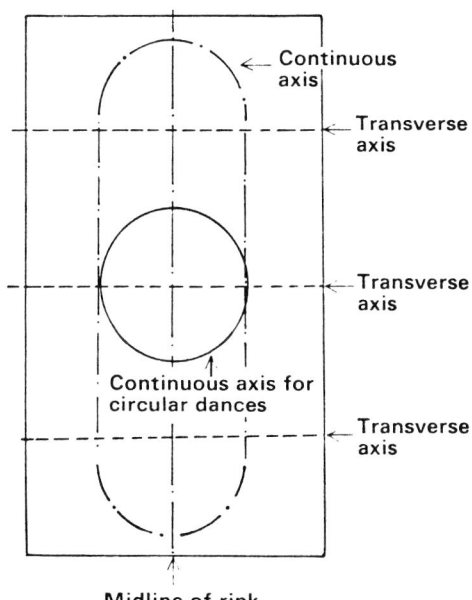

Placement of dance steps and edges on a rink must conform to patterns.

keep in time to the music but uses it to harmonise the skating movements (jumps, spins, spirals, etc.,) into one rhythmic whole. So, *on the rink* practise running, stroking and curving to the music; *off the rink*, listen to music and even try to visualize skating to it – walk about at home and try to keep time to the music. After a while, no matter what the music is, whether film or television music, classical or pop, you will suddenly find yourself thinking, 'I'm going to skate to that' – you will then be well on the way to bcoming an *interesting* skater, as opposed to the constant lapper round the rink.

Just as the figure skater has to learn about the long and transverse axes for his figures, so, too, the dancer has to learn the terminology about placement of the dance steps. Reference will be made to the rink '*midline*' – this is, as it suggests, an imaginary line running the length of the rink and bisecting it into two equal parts (see diagram). The *continuous axis* is the imaginary line which runs around the rink in relation to which the pattern of the dance is made. Thus, in circular dances the continuous axis is a circle, and in other dances it usually consists of two straight lines down each side of the rink connected by semi-circles at each end. As in figures, the *transverse axis* is that which intersects the continuous axis at right-angles.

It is at this stage that you will find the disciplines diverging: dancing, on the one hand, requiring a partner, and figure skating, on the other, which may be performed solo, though a partner is necessary for pair figure skating. With the acquisition of easy, sure movements over the rink in time to music, we now turn our attention to the 'school' or 'compulsory' figures previously referred to.

5. The Basic Eights

There are four basic circle eights. These are: forward outside, forward inside, backward outside, and backward inside. They are performed on either foot.

FORWARD OUTSIDE EIGHT (Rfo-Lfo)

This figure, known as the Curve Eight, is performed on one foot on each half of the figure. That is, the first circle is skated on the right foot and the second circle on the left foot (see diagram). The abbreviation for skating this figure is: Curve Eight Rfo-Lfo.

When skating these Eights, no preliminary steps are allowed to gain impetus – they must be started from 'rest' and the *stroke must be clean and taken from the side of the blade, not from the toe*. No exaggerated posture or contortion of the body is permitted. When one circle has been completed and the skater is about to commence the second, the change from right to left skating foot (or vice versa) must be made without any pause.

Take up your position at the point where the two imaginary circles will meet to form the eight. Your right foot should be pointed in the starting direction of the circle and your left foot at right-angles, so that a good push-off can be made. Turn your body sideways so that you are in Position A, i.e. your right shoulder must be leading, with your left shoulder held well back. Your right hip will be forward and your left hip held back. In other words, you are sideways to the motion. Now thrust from your left skate with a slightly bent right knee, extending your left leg. As you start on the curve, your left leg should be kept slightly bent and over the line your right skate is making. Keep your head up and look over your right shoulder at your line of travel.

Once you have started on your edge, keep your right knee or tracing knee relaxed and slightly bent. Because your skating position has to be completely reversed by the time you complete the circle, so that you may strike out properly on the left foot, you must gradually start to shift your body and arms into the new position. Hold Position A until you have gone about one-third the way round the circle, then gradually bring your left leg (the free leg) forward. Do not move your hips. Continue to bring your left foot forward until it passes your right foot and is extended in front and over the imaginary skating tracing. About two-thirds of the way round the circle, bring your arms and shoulders round so that your right arm and shoulder commence to rotate back, and your left arm and shoulder come forward, and also gradually bring your free (left) hip forwards, ending in Position B.

You will now, at the completion of the first circle, be in the correct position to commence the second. This second circle is done in exactly the same way as the first one. Each figure, in tests and competitions, has to be skated three times, so when the second time round is commenced on the right foot this is termed 're-tracing' the figure.

There are certain rules which must be adhered to: the area where the change from one foot to the other is made must be kept to a minimum; circles must not overlap; curves have to be skated without wobbles or sub-curves; curves or circle must be uniform in size, and long and transverse axes must be maintained. As you become more proficient, you must strive to trace the figure laid down without sacrificing position.

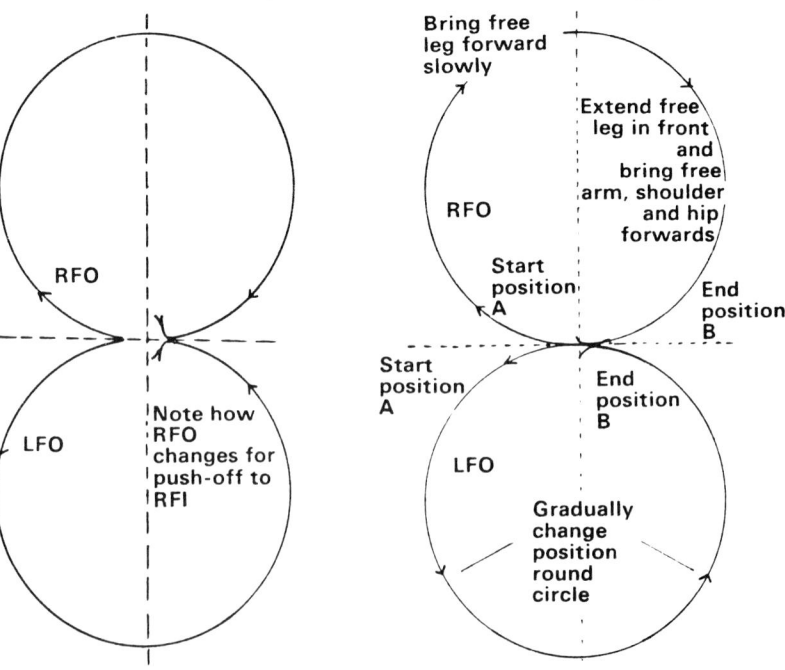

Rfo-Lfo circle eight.   Rfo-Lfo circle eight body positions.

You will find it helpful at this stage to trace the illustrations showing the four basic positions A, B, C and D on to a thin card. Then cut out the skating figures or leave them on a narrow piece of card. Bend a base under or add a small tab at the back; then draw out the circles on a sheet of paper and place the appropriate cut-out in its correct place on the circle. By doing this and also by taking up the positions in front of a mirror, when practising 'dry', you will soon become familiar with the correct skating positions.

Though we have referred to four basic skating positions, you will find in practice that the forward outside edge uses Positions A and B, the outside back uses B and A in that order, and the inside back uses B and A in that order, whilst the inside forward uses C and D in that sequence. The edges do, of course, use all the positions, notably C and D, for executing certain turns and advanced movements.

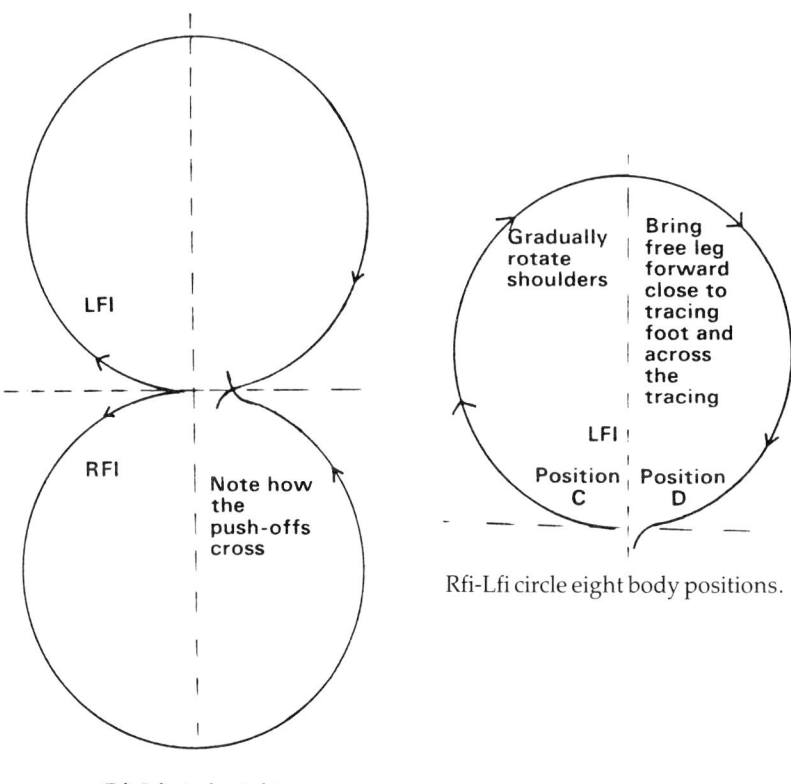

Rfi-Lfi circle eight.

Rfi-Lfi circle eight body positions.

FORWARD INSIDE EIGHT (Ffi-Lfi)

This figure uses Positions C and D for commencement and completion of the circle (see diagram). In the Forward Outside Eight you started with your back to the circle so that you were leaning to the outside. In the Forward Inside Eight the lean is to the inside. The starting foot is the right foot, but the direction this time is anti-clockwise.

Take up your starting position with your right foot pointing in the direction of the curve to be skated. Position C is assumed with your right shoulder, arm, free leg and hip back. Your left arm will be leading. Look forwards and slightly over your left shoulder. Push off and hold this position until you have completed the first ⅓ of the circle, at which point you gradually rotate your shoulders so that your right arm leads (see diagram). During this rotation, your hips remain stationary. Approaching the final ⅓ of the circle and preparing for the change of foot, your left leg should slowly come forward close to your skating foot and turn out so that it lies across the print you are going to make. Your hips gradually assume a forward position and, as you approach the close of the first circle, your left foot should be ready to be placed on the ice on to the left forward inside edge. Thus you will already be in reversed position, ready to strike off into the second circle on your left skate.

BACK OUTSIDE EIGHT (Rbo-Lbo)

The main difficulty in skating this figure lies in the complicated push-off required.

Take up your position to commence the figure with both feet on the rink, with your full weight on the left skate. Your right foot should be slightly further forward than your left foot, with the toe pointing downwards and just resting on the rink surface. Assume a position in which your left shoulder is drawn back and your right is forward, bend your left knee strongly and then push off backwards on to your right skate (see diagram). As soon as the strike is made, lift your left foot. You should be looking over your left shoulder and your hips should be square. For a brief moment, your shoulders will be perpendicular to the tracing and your left leg should be held fairly close to your skating leg. Now reverse your shoulders and assume position B, with your tracing shoulder and arm (right) back, whilst your free (left) shoulder, arm, hip and leg are forwards. You now look over your right shoulder. About half-way round the circle, you have to prepare to make the second circle.

Gradually assume Position A with your free shoulder, arm, leg and hip drawn back and your right (tracing) shoulder and arm forwards.

When the circle is completed, your shoulders should be parallel to the transverse axis, ready for the push-off on your left foot. To prevent over-rotation, allow your shoulders to relax from the parallel position, and bring your left foot to the starting point and push-off from your right foot. The striking position should be identical with the original push-off from rest. Make certain that you close your circles, i.e. bring the first circle right up to the start of the second one and, above all, do not double-track, that is skate part of the change-over from one circle to the other with both skates on the rink.

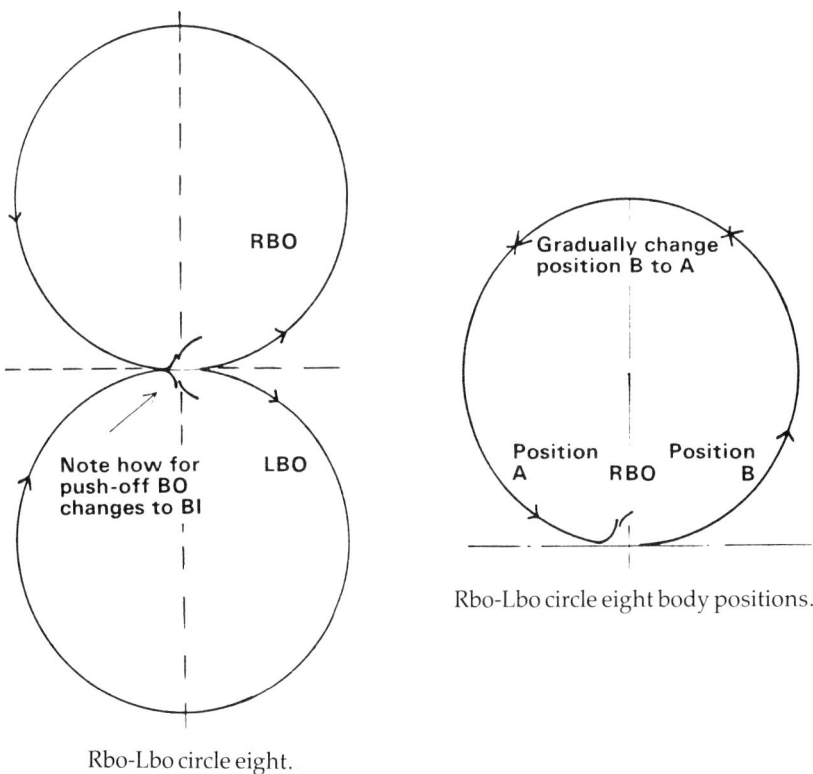

Rbo-Lbo circle eight.

Rbo-Lbo circle eight body positions.

BACK INSIDE EIGHT (Rbi-Lfi)

The push-off for this figure (see diagram) is much the same as for the Back Outside Eight, except that you lean inwards over the skate. It is important that you pick up your left skate immediately and that your right blade catches a very definite inside edge. Adopt position B for two-thirds of the circle then gradually assume position A. Remember, however, to change the position of your head (see diagram).

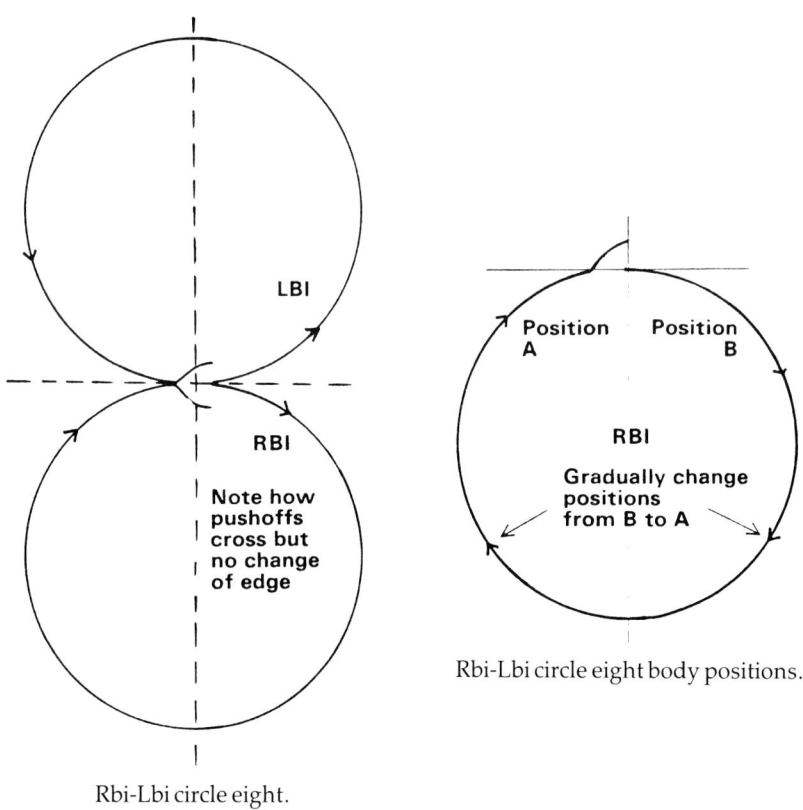

Rbi-Lbi circle eight.

Rbi-Lbi circle eight body positions.

CHANGES OF EDGE

These may be defined as movements performed on one foot in which the skater changes from one edge to the other.

Changes of edge are of two types (see diagram): the three-lobed serpentine figure and the two-circle Eight skated on one foot (the one-foot Eight) which is a rather advanced figure. The change of edge serpentine, which consists of a half-circle on to the opposite edge for a full circle, then a change of foot followed by a half-circle, change, and full circle, is the next step in skating edges.

Changes of edge are used in free skating to link movements and also in dancing, where a change can be very slight indeed. Very advanced figures incorporate a change in their structure, e.g. loop-change-loop, change edge double loop, change bracket.

Basically, the change of edge consists of one half of a Curve Eight with the change of body and leg position and preparation for the thrust on to the other leg carried out on one foot only. A good rise and fall on the skating knee is essential, and the whole character of a good change of edge depends on the incorporation of the bending and straightening of the skating knee before, during, and after the change, with the correct body positions. If you are already able to skate the Curve Eights correctly, the changes of edge should present no difficulties.

FORWARD CHANGES OF EDGE (Rfoi-Lfio : Lfoi-Rfio)

Start the first semi-circle on the forward outside edge as for the Curve Eight, but, instead of waiting until you are well round the circle before you bring your free leg forward, slowly bring your free leg past your skating leg at one-quarter of the circle. Do not move your shoulders.

When the semi-circle has been skated on the outside edge, you change your lean from out of the completed half-circle into the circle about to be made. This is done by taking up the position of the start of an Inside Forward Eight, i.e. with your free shoulder and arm leading. The actual change will be little more than a skate's length and this should be straight along the tangent of the two circles. There will, at first, be either or both of two tendencies: to go out of line either by curving in too much, or by skating at an angle across the tangent. A simple exercise to correct this error, using the free leg and foot, is easily learned. At one-quarter of the circle, swing your free foot so that first of all it points towards the centre of the circle after the change of edge. Your free leg should be fully extended just before the change itself. At the moment of change, swing your free leg back towards the centre of the completed half-circle. After the change, you complete the inner-edge circle, just as you would the ordinary Inside Forward Eight.

Having completed the first half of the figure (Rfoi), you now commence the next half of the figure (Lfio). Make a normal push-off on to the inside forward edge. A quarter of the way round the circle, bring your free leg forward and at the same time reverse your shoulders so that your body position is identical with that at the completion of the simple inside curve.

Make the change at the completion of the half-circle. Bring your free leg up in front and then back, and at the same time reverse your

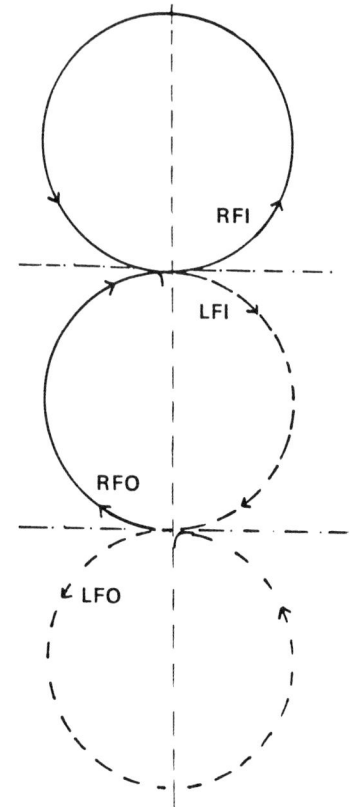

Change of edge: Rfoi-Lfio.

shoulders. You will now be on an outside edge. The body position is different from starting the normal outside edge and approximates to the final position of the ordinary Outside Edge Eight. You must hold this position throughout the whole of the circle, but bring your free leg forward during the last ⅓ of the circle so that you will be ready to take-off on to the forward outside edge on the other foot and commence the figure over again.

BACKWARD CHANGES OF EDGE (Rboi-Lbio : Lboi-Rbio)

These are more difficult than the forward changes. You must use the same basic principles of change, and the use of the free leg is similar to that in forward changes. After the push-off on to the back outside edge, which is done in the normal way, keep your free leg close to your tracing leg and keep your tracing arm and shoulder forward. But, here is the main difference: do *not* look over your free shoulder – look to the inside of the circle you are making towards the spot where the change will be made.

On commencing the second half of the figure on the back inside edge, hold the circle as in the ordinary figure, with your free leg passing your skating leg at the ¼ mark of the first circle. Swing your free leg over the tracing you are about to make, then lift your skating shoulder slightly higher and hold it there until after the change is made. The moment you are on the outside edge, lower this shoulder, swing your free leg back, and stretch your free arm across your chest. You must hold this position (which checks the body and holds it on the edge properly) until you are ⅔ round the circle, then gradually take up the position of an ordinary back outside edge and hold this till the close of the circle.

These changes of edge should first be practised 'in field' to acquire smoothness of movement and the necessary soft knee action, and to practise the different head positions involved.

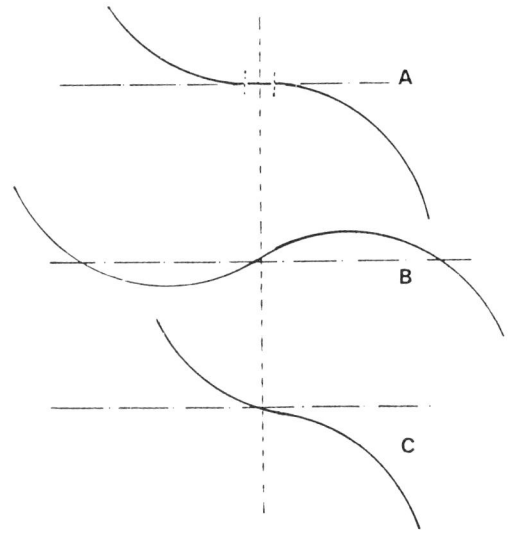

(A) Correct change of edge; (B and C) incorrect tracings.

Important

No matter what session you are skating in, whether private or public, you should make it a definite and rigid rule to practise your four simple edges *every time you skate* and to concentrate on neatness of footwork. Neatness of footwork and softness in the knee action cannot too strongly be emphasised. Remember, too, to keep your arms low. All too often one sees experienced skaters, skate dancers usually, who stretch their arms out in line with their shoulders. This is not necessary and does, in fact, look slightly ridiculous!

6. Turns

There are a limited number of turns in skating – they are divided into:

(a) One-footed movements in which the skater turns from forwards to backwards (or vice versa) whilst skating continuously on one foot.

(b) Two-footed movements in which a change from forwards to backwards (or vice versa) is accomplished with a change of foot.

ONE-FOOTED MOVEMENTS

These may involve a change of direction accompanied by an unchanged character of edge, e.g. from an outside forward edge to an outside back edge, or accompanied by a change of character of edge, e.g. from an outside forward edge to an inside back edge. There are also rotational changes to take into account. A natural rotation is one in which the body turns in the same direction as the curve being traced. A reverse rotation is one in which the body turns contrary to the direction of the tracing curve.

One-footed turns are: Three Turns, Brackets, Counters and Rockers. You will only be concerned with the Three Turns performed on an outside forward edge to an inside back edge. The other turns are more advanced and require tuition from a professional coach. But, for the record, we shall identify the turns.

The Three Turn

The diagram shows this turn on one foot, changing the direction of the skating from forwards to backwards, or backwards to forwards, and

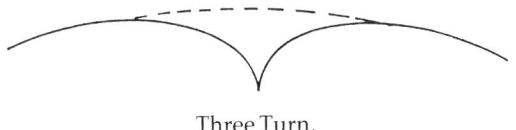

Three Turn.

accompanied by a change of character of the edges. The rotation is natural and follows the curve of the circle. The edges change from inside to outside, or from outside to inside.

The Rocker

The diagram shows a change of direction as in the Three Turn with a natural rotation for the first curve; the following unchanged character of edge in the second circle has a change of rotation.

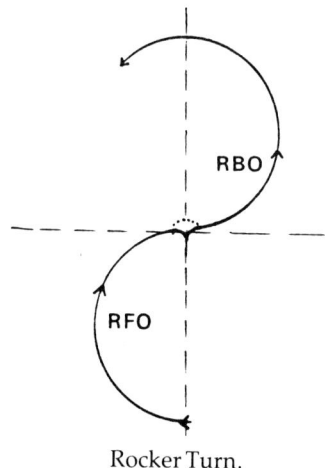

Rocker Turn.

The Bracket

This is performed on one foot (diagram), as in the Three Turn, but the turn is made against the natural rotation of the curve, i.e. the edges are of different character and the turn is reversed.

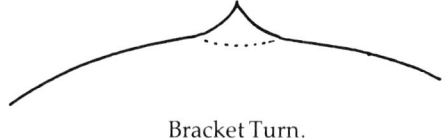

Bracket Turn.

The Counter

This, as the name suggests, involves a counter or reverse direction of rotation. This is a change of direction from forwards to backwards, or from backwards to forwards, and is the reverse of the Rocker in that the two symmetrical curves forming the figure are skated with the turn in a

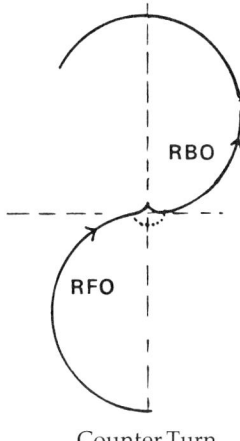

Counter Turn.

reverse rotation, whilst the second has a natural sense of rotation. The edges are of the same character.

The abbreviations used to describe these Turns are as follows: T = Three; RK = Rocker; C = Counter; B = Bracket. Coupled with the abbreviations noted earlier, the following abbreviations would indicate:

RfoTbi = Right forward outside Three to back inside edge.
RfiBbi = Right forward inside Bracket to back inside edge.
LfoRKbo = Left forward outside Rocker to back outside edge.

One footed turns are incorporated in the Compulsory Figures and are featured in the Schedules of Figures. They are skated in eight or paragraph form, and in the very advanced figures may also incoporate two different kinds of turn, e.g. Bracket-Rocker-Bracket.

TWO-FOOTED MOVEMENTS

These moves are simpler to define. They are, basically, the *Mohawk*, which involves a change from forwards to backwards or backwards to forwards with edges of the same character. *Mohawks* are divided into the following categories:

Closed Mohawk

This is a Mohawk skated with tracings crossing, but with the feet not crossed. The free foot is placed on the rink along the outer edge of the

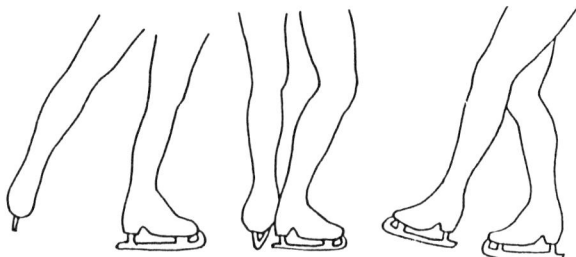

The 'Closed Mohawk' movement
Direction of skating – left to right. A left forward outside closed mohawk to right back outside. Note that the hips are in the closed position with free leg trailing after the turn.

heel of the tracing foot. When the weight is taken on to the new skating foot, the free foot is in front of the toe of the tracing foot. The hip position is closed.

Open Mohawk

A Mohawk is performed by placing the free foot by the inside of the ankle of the tracing foot, the weight is transferred to the new skating foot and the foot that is now free is carried behind the heel of the skating foot. The open hip position which follows gives the Open Mohawk its name.

Mohawk turns are also classified as *Crossed* and *Uncrossed*. A *Crossed Mohawk* is one where the feet are crossed in front or behind, but the tracings do not cross. An *Uncrossed Mohawk* is one where the tracings cross, but the feet do not.

Swing Mohawk

This is an uncrossed type in which the free leg is swung forward past the tracing foot and brought back close to it, before changing feet. It may be Open or Closed.

Choctaw

This two-footed movement is a Turn from forwards to backwards (or vice versa) from one foot to another on edges of different character, e.g. outside to inside. The Choctaws are *Crossed, Uncrossed, Closed, Open* and *Swing*, as in the case of the Mohawks.

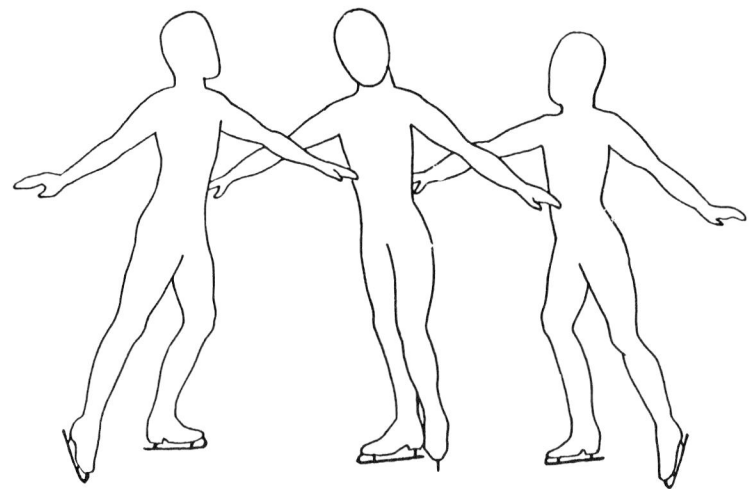

Sequence for 'Open Mohawk'. Direction of skating left to right. Commence on left forward inside edge (A), right foot brought to instep of skating foot (B), weight placed on right foot which continues in backward inside edge with left (free) foot leading (C). Note the open hip position from which the turn gets its name.

SKATING THE TURNS

Forward Outside Three

During this Turn you will skate from an outside forward edge to an inside back edge, rotating in the direction of travel. This is a very important turn because, if done badly, it can be just about the ugliest movement on ice.

Let us learn the Three Turn on the left foot first, because you will be following the direction of the rink skating.

Take up your T-position. Commence the figure as if you were skating a forward outside edge. Now hold your skating hip underneath you so that you can feel your weight going through it down to the skating foot. Press your free leg and hip back. Stand perfectly erect. There must be no lean other than into the circle. Now rotate your shoulders against your hips until you are skating with your free shoulder leading strongly. At this point, lower your free leg and foot so that, with the skate off the rink, they assume a T-position behind your left foot. Try to touch your free foot against the heel of your skating foot and, as you still increase the rotation of your skating shoulder, allow your weight to transfer momentarily to the ball of your foot. Your skate will lift at the back slightly and turn through 180° to backwards. As soon as your skate takes up the inside back edge, reverse your shoulder pressure, press your free hip and shoulder back, and lean inwards on to the edge.

The action of the knee of the skating leg is vitally important. You push off on to a strongly bent skating knee, then straighten your leg as you come to the turn. As your feet come together in the T-position, both knees should be straight. After the turn, when the inside back edge is assumed, you bend your skating knee again.

The body action is really quite simple: begin the turn with your skating side leading and end it with your free side leading. Your skating shoulder should should be kept slightly down and the actual turn should be done very quickly.

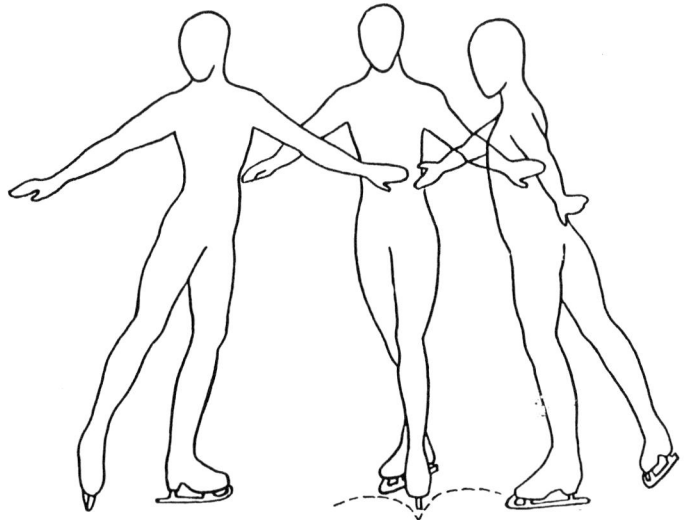

The 'Three Turn'. In this drawing the skater approaches the turn of a left forward outside edge and turns to a backward inside edge of the same foot. Direction of skating ←

Inside Mohawk

This is probably the simplest of all Turns to learn. You commence with an inside forward edge on one foot and step on to the inside backward edge of the other foot.

Begin, as usual, in the T-position. Push off on to an inside forward edge, keeping your skating knee well bent. As you will be skating on your right foot for this lesson, press your left shoulder, arm, and free foot back over the tracing edge. Now draw your free foot towards the heel of your right foot, at the same time bending your free knee. Your toes should be turned out as much as possible so that your heels are drawn together. Touch the inside of your skating heel with your free heel. Now, reverse the pressure against your shoulders and allow your body to turn to the left. Quickly transfer your weight on to your left skate and at the same time slide your right skate away, in the direction of travel. Maintain a constant and steady lean to the inside of the circle.

The Mohawk which you have just skated is an Open Mohawk and is used in dance skating and extensively in free skating.

7. Dance Skating (Simple Dances)

As explained earlier, dance skating consists of a series of set steps rather like Old Tyme and sequence dancing in a ballroom.

It is necessary first of all to find a partner who will suit you for height, weight, and skating ability. Nothing looks more ridiculous than a tall man trying to ice skate with a tiny girl partner, or a small man being pulled along by a strong, well-built female! During the public sessions and at club sessions you will, of course, skate with a variety of partners, from experts to downright novices. However, to get the maximum enjoyment and benefit from dance skating partners should 'match' both physically and in skating ability.

Before attempting to dance with each other, you should spend considerable time running round the rink together in time to different rhythms. The correct holds should be learned and the couple should move round the rink together, using the various holds, occasionally changing from side to side. Because two people are skating together, the need to hold free legs over the tracing becomes apparent, as legs pushed out to the side soon trip a hapless partner and bring both parties to earth with a crash.

You and your partner should strive for the same knee action, your heads must move neatly and in unison, and the whole effect should be effortless. Footwork, too, must be neat, and free legs and feet should match in height from the rink.

Movements such as Three Turns, chassés, etc., should be practised together with the extended arm hold so that distance can be maintained and yet you will always be 'in touch'. The man must be prepared to show off his lady to advantage and become a background figure; this is also essential in pair skating.

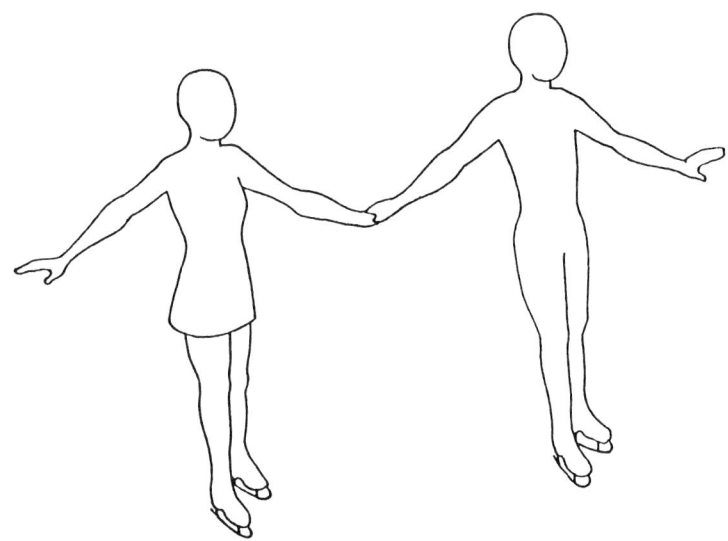

Hand-in-Hand hold, used prior to commencing a dance, also used in Pair Skating. Partners may be on either side.

THE DANCE HOLDS

Hand in Hand

In this position the couple face the same direction and skate side by side (illustration). It is customary for the lady to be on the man's right.

Waltz Hold

This is also termed the 'closed' position. Partners face each other, one skating forwards, the other backwards. The man's right hand is placed firmly against the lady's back at the shoulderblade with the elbow raised and bent. She places her left hand on his right shoulder. The man's left arm and the lady's right arm are extended at shoulder height (see photograph).

Foxtrot Hold

This hold is sometimes called the 'open' position. Here the Waltz hold is used but the partners open into a V-position and skate in the same direction. This is rather like the Promenade position in ballroom dancing.

(*Left*) The Waltz hold.
(*Right*) Bad posture in this waltz hold is shown with the extended arms too high and the boy's fingers spread apart against his partner's back. Two very common faults!

Tango Hold

In this hold the partners face in opposite directions. The hold is similar to the Waltz hold, but the partners do not skate directly opposite each other. They skate hip to hip, with the man on the left or the right of the lady. This is sometimes termed the 'outside' position.

Kilian Hold

The partners skate in the same direction, facing the same way. The man is on the lady's left, with her left shoulder against his right shoulder.

Reversed Kilian Hold

This is identical to the Kilian Hold described above except that the man is on the lady's right. The Fiesta Tango is danced in this hold.

It should be pointed out that dances should be skated with as much expression as possible, edges should be strong, and you should show true rhythmic feeling, but, at the same time, the prescribed relationship of the edges to the patterns laid down must be maintained. When you dance on ice skates, show that you are enjoying yourself and be as relaxed as if you were dancing at a party or in a ballroom.

The four dance holds shown above are (*top left*) Kilian hold used in both ice dancing and pair skating (*top right*) Reversed Kilian. (*Bottom left*) Foxtrot Hold (*Bottom right*) Tango Hold.

THE GLIDE WALTZ

The Glide Waltz is a very easy and pleasant dance to learn. Both partners do the same steps and skate forward in the Kilian Hold, that is, side by side. The pattern of the dance is serpentine, and open chassés are used on alternate feet. This dance is a useful exercise for the Preliminary Waltz (or Waltz Movement) Dance in the Preliminary Dance Test of the National Skating Association. It is a good exercise in skating in time to the music, with a good rise and fall of the skating knee.

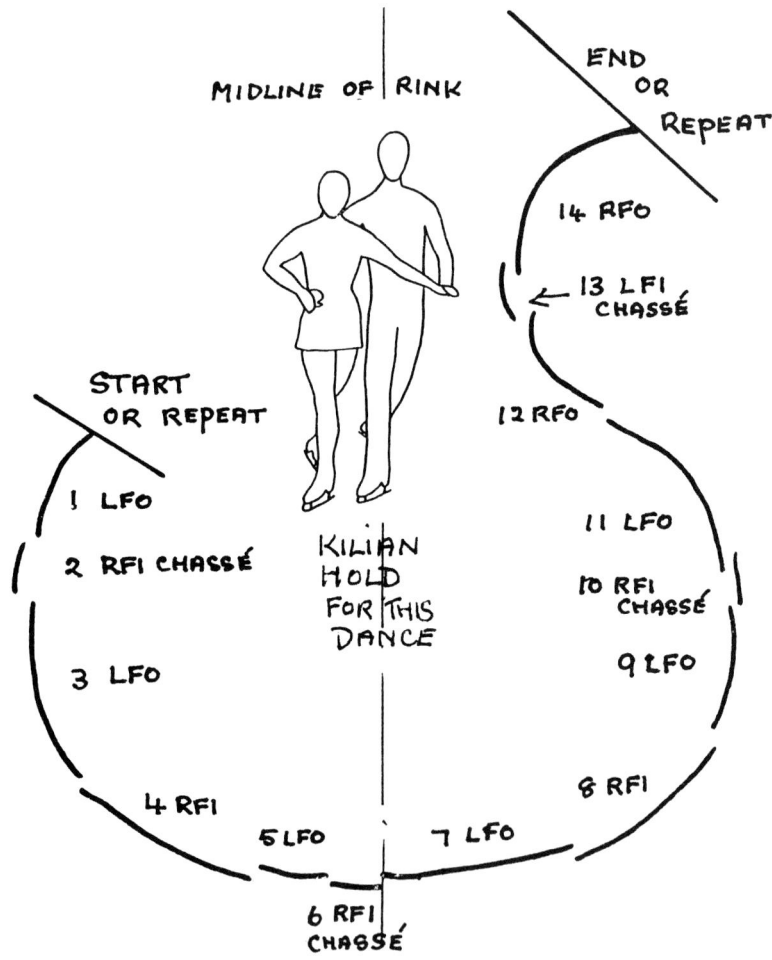

Dance hold, pattern, and steps for the 'Glide Waltz'.

At the ends of the rink the chassé steps are not skated but the couple skate on right forward inside edges round the corners.

The couple should skate with their bodies at more or less 90° to the skating pattern throughout the dance.

After preliminary opening steps consisting of 3-beat edges on left and right foot respectively, the dance commences with a chassé to the left followed by a 3-beat edge on the left forward outside edge: then follows a chassé begun on the right forward outside edge followed by an outside forward edge on the right foot. The corner steps consist of a chassé (Lfo:Rfi) followed by a right inside forward edge which is held for 3 beats. A further right inside forward edge may be executed following a further chassé if the width of the rink requires it.

Your free foot must never come ahead of the skating foot. Carriage must be upright, with erect head, and the toe of the free foot must be turned outwards and downwards.

The timing of the open chassé, in waltz tempo, are shown below, and the pattern of the dance and placement of steps on the ice is shown in the dance plan.

The steps of the Glide Waltz are as follows:

Step No.	Description	Beats of music

Steps 1 to 4 are an opening chassé movement aimed at the barrier: this is known as a *corner sequence*.

1	Lfo	2
2	Rfi open chassé	1
3	Lfo	3
4	Rfi	3

Steps 5 to 8, a repeat of corner sequence, with barrier lobe.

5	Lfo	2
6	Rfi open chassé	1
7	Lfo	3
8	Rfi	3

Step 9 commences a barrier lobe aimed along the straight of the rink.

9	Lfo	2
10	Rfi open chassé	1
11	Lfo	3

From step 11 there is a change of body lean, called a *rockover*, in order to prepare for the centre lobe right forward outside edge.

12	Rfo aimed at centre	2
13	Lfi open chassé	1
14	Rfo aiming towards barrier	3

Steps 12-13-14 may be repeated again following a repetition of steps 9-10-11 if the length of the rink warrants it.

THE FOXTROT MOVEMENT

This is also called the Preliminary Foxtrot and forms a compulsory dance for candidates in the Preliminary Dance Test organized by the National Skating Association of Great Britain.

This dance is very simple, though it is a real test of skating proper edges with good style and carriage. During the dancing you must extend your free leg properly and see that your tracing leg bends and straightens well. The Foxtrot Movement is very pleasant to skate as a dance in its own right. It has the great advantage that both partners skate the same steps, which are forward only. Preliminary opening steps are allowed, not exceeding four, after which the dance starts. The tempo is 26 bars per minute in Foxtrot 4/4.

You and your partner assume the Kilian hold, with the lady on the man's right. After the preliminary steps have been completed, strike

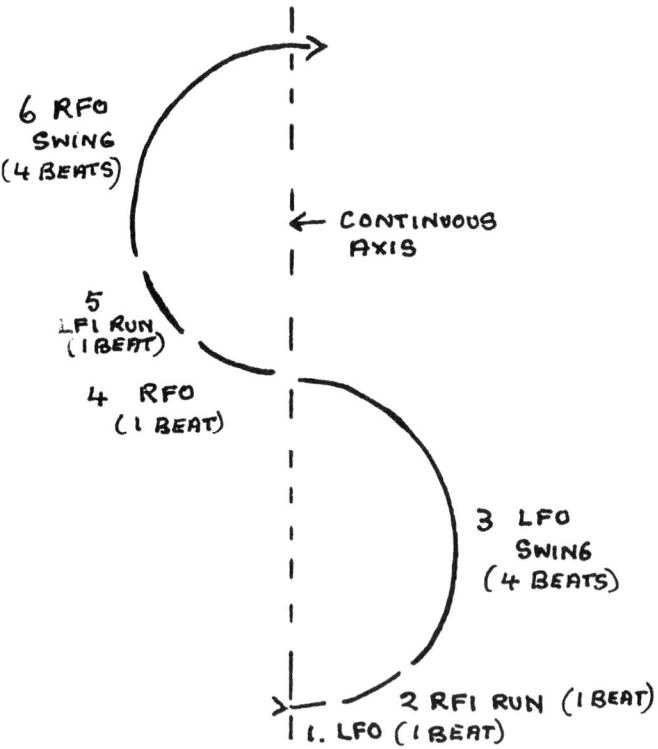

Steps and pattern of the 'Foxtrot Movement'.

on to a left forward outside edge, followed by a right inside forward run and a left outside forward edge. On this step, both of you swing your free leg slowly forward, past your tracing feet. The edge is steepened and your skating legs should be bent. The next step is taken on to the right forward outside edge, followed by a left inside run, then a strong right forward outside edge and a forward swing of the left leg. The runs and swings are repeated alternately on each foot. The timing is 1:1:4 (left forward outside edge 1:right forward inside edge 1:left forward outside 4 – and so on alternately).

The couple should look towards the centre of the rink when skating on the left outside edge, and towards the barrier when skating the right forward inside edge.

It is excellent exercise to practise the Foxtrot Movement backwards in which you perform backwards progressives or runs, followed by an outside back edge during which the free foot is swung back slowly. You can also alternate skating backwards and forwards in Waltz Position.

Steps of the Foxtrot Movement

Step No.	Description	Beats of music
1	Lfo	1
2	Rfi Run (Progressive)	1
3	Lfo swing free leg to front, returning to side of skating foot at commencement of beat 4	4
4	Rfo	1
5	Lfi Run (Progressive)	1
6	Rfo Swing free leg as on step 3	4

Refer to the diagram for steps and timing of the Foxtrot Movement.

8. More Advanced Dances

When you have successfully performed the simple steps of the elementary dances, it will be very useful if you and your partner learn each other's steps because, when you each begin to skate different steps, dancing becomes a little more complicated.

In order to link the various elements of skate dancing together you will find it helpful to learn the following dance, which makes use of runs or progressives, cross-rolls, inside edges, and swinging the free leg. It is skated to Foxtrot music in the Kilian hold with the lady on the man's right. The steps are the same for both partners and care must be taken when swinging the free leg to make sure that both partners' legs match.

THE OLYMPIC FOXTROT

Commence with the usual opening steps. The first step of the dance is a LFO of 1 beat followed by a run or progressive on RFI for 1 beat. Step 3 is LFO for two beats followed by step 4 which is a cross roll (RFO over left foot) for 2 beats, then step 5 which is a cross roll on LFO for 2 beats. Step 6 commences with a cross roll (RFO over left) which is held for 4 beats: during this the left leg is slowly swung forward on the third beat. Steps 7, 8 and 9 are repeats of the opening steps 1, 2 and 3, after which step 10 is skated on RFI for 2 beats followed by step 11 LFI for 2 beats. The dance sequence ends with RFI of 4 beats during which the free left leg is slowly swung forward on the third beat.

In this dance the cross rolled edges have to be skated boldly and the three inside edges have to be struck from the side. It is important that you and your partner keep close together and do not part at the hips.

Steps

Step No.	Description	Beats of music
1	Lfo	1
2	Rfi Run (Progressive)	1

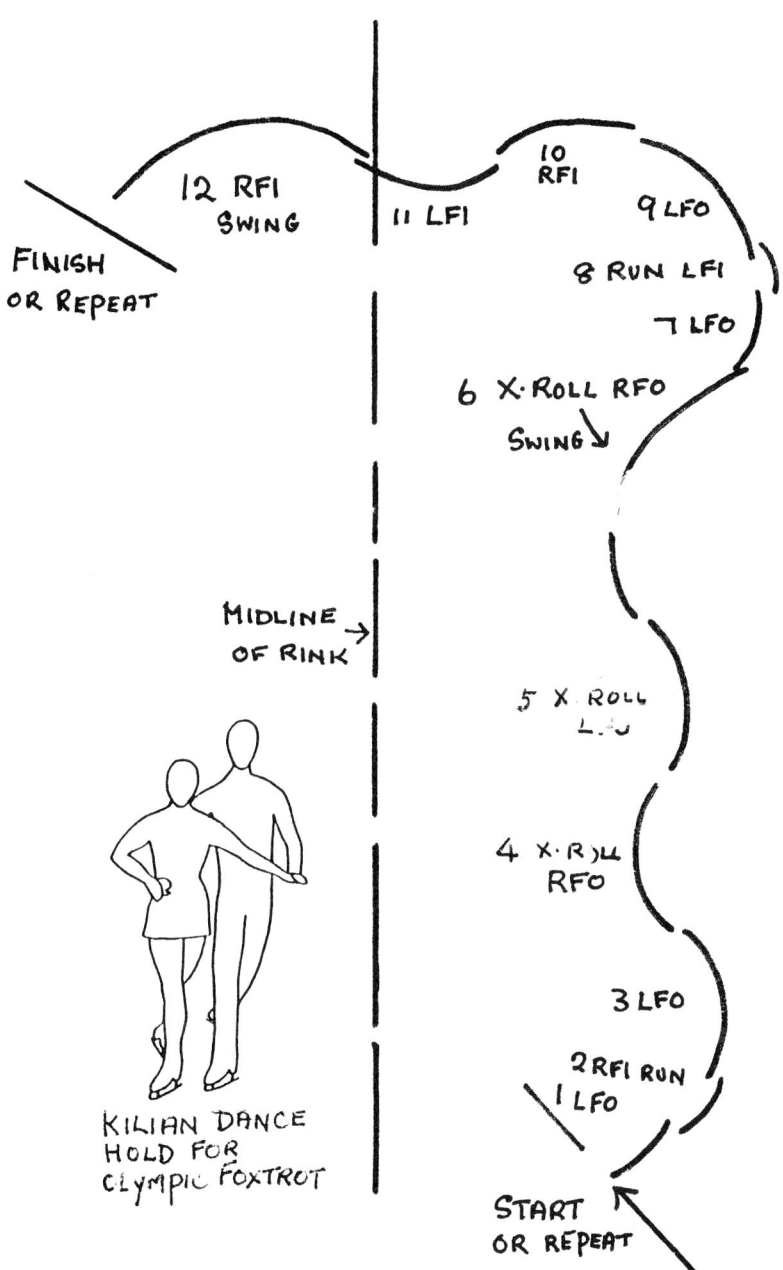

Dance hold, pattern, and steps for the 'Olympic Foxtrot'.

Step No.	Description	Beats of Music
3	Lfo	2
4	Rfo Cross Roll	2
5	Lfo Cross Roll	2
6	Rfo Cross Roll – swing the free leg through on count 3	4
7	Lfo	1
8	Rfi Run (Progressive)	1
9	Lfo	2
10	Rfi	2
11	Lfi	2
12	Rfi Swing free leg through on count 3	4

Steps 4, 5 and 6 should be skated strongly.

THE WALTZ MOVEMENT

This is also known as the Preliminary Waltz and is skated in the Preliminary Dance Test. It is skated in the waltz hold at waltz tempo 3/4 time at 45 bars per minute. Basically it consists of forward and backward open chassé movements, and includes a three turn executed on the left forward outside edge. Steps are identical for lady and man. There are 14 steps in a sequence which are alternated. Steps 1-7 skated by the man are skated 8-14 by the lady: then skated 8-14 by the man and 1-7 by the lady. See list of steps.

    The backward chassé movement is based on the same technique as the forward chassé. The partners face each other and when the man executes a forward chassé the lady executes a back one, and vice versa. The chassé commences with the skater holding a backward outside edge with the free foot extended in front, that is, trailing. The free foot is then returned to the skating foot which is momentarily lifted for 1 beat and then replaced. The free leg is then again extended to its trailing position.

    The dance is a succession of barrier and centre of rink lobes and has no set pattern or sequence though the National Skating Association allow a minimum of two open chassés and a maximum of four open chassés before the man makes his three turn (the lady skates the same number of chassés backwards). As the man executes his three turn and steps on to the backward outside edge the lady executes a step to forwards from backwards on a left forward outside edge. There are two beats of music before the turn and one beat after.

Steps

Step No.	Man	Description Lady	Beats of music
1	Rfo	Lbo	2

Step No.	Man	Description Lady	Beats of Music
2	Lfi chassé	Rbi chassé	1
3	Rfo	Lbo	3
4	Lfo	Rbo	2
5	Rfi chassé	Lbi chassé	1
6	Lfo Three turn to Lbi	Rbo	3
7	Rbo	Lfo	3
8	Lbo	Rfo	2
9	Rbi chassé	Lfi chassé	1
10	Lbo	Rfo	3
11	Rbo	Lfo	2
12	Lbi chassé	Rfi chassé	1
13	Rbo	Lfo Three turn to Lbi	3
14	Lfo	Rbo	3
Repeat			

THE EUROPEAN WALTZ

This is an International Dance which, although the steps are simple enough, is extremely difficult to learn correctly. You either skate it very badly or very well – it is that type of dance!

Basically the European Waltz consists of a Three Turn on the outside edge forwards, and of outside edges. The dance is skated in the Waltz

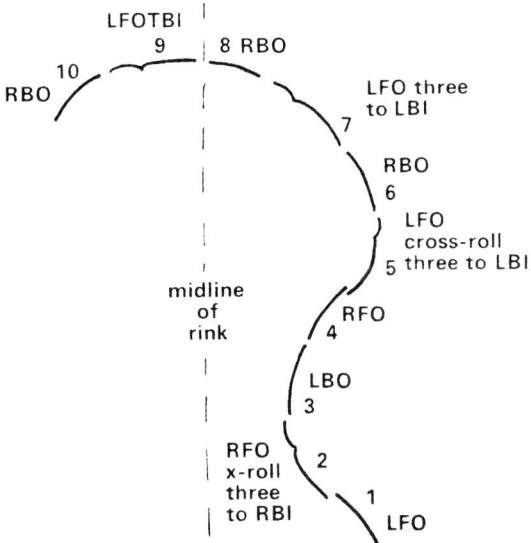

Pattern and steps for gentleman in European Waltz.

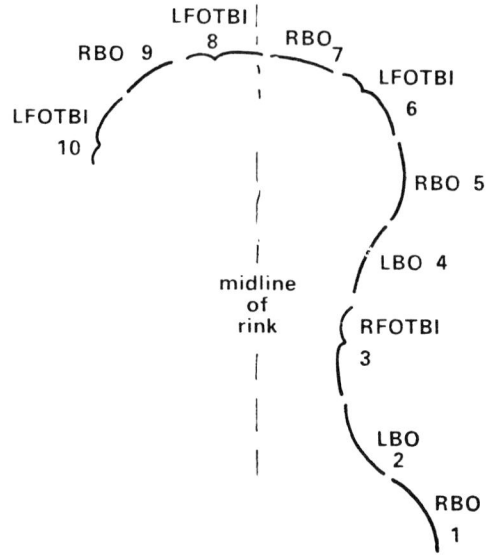

Steps for lady in European Waltz; quarter rink pattern.

position and the man must skate directly facing his partner throughout the dance on all strokes. The free foot must be kept close to the skating foot and, as the dance is skated in a series of lobes, those skated along the rink should be semi-circles. The number of lobes skated depends upon the length of the rink.

Table of Steps

The rotation of the partners must be well controlled and should be continuous throughout each lobe and at the beginning of each new lobe it is reversed. Keeping the free foot close to the skating foot helps to keep the rotation under control. There is often discussion as to how many three turns should be skated round the end of the rink. This depends, of course, on the width of the skating area and may vary from 4 to 6, though on very narrow rinks only 3 many be possible. Turns must be made between the partner's feet and to achieve this it is necessary to skate towards each other.

Steps of European Waltz

Step No.	Man	Description Beats of music	Lady	Beats of music
1	Lfo	3	Rbo	3

Step No.	Man	Beats of music	Lady	Beats of music
2	Rfo Cross roll	2	Lbo	3
	Three turn to Rbi	1		
3	Lbo	3	Rfo	2
			Three turn to Rbi	1
4	Rfo	3	Lbo	3
5	Lfo Cross roll	2	Rbo	3
	Three turn to Lbi	1		
6	Rbo	3	Lfo	2
			Three turn to Lbi	1
7	Lfo	2	Rbo	3
	Three turn to Lbi	1		
8	Rbo	3	Lfo	2
			Three turn to Lbi	1
9	Lfo	2	Rbo	3
	Three turn to Lbi	1		
10	Rbo	3	Lfo	2
			Three turn to Lbi	1
11	Lfo	2	Rbo	3
	Three turn to Lbi	1		
12	Lbo	3	Lfo	2
			Three turn to Lbi	1

Sequences recommence with step 1. This list of steps is for a three lobe pattern dance.

Faults to avoid

It is a horrible sight to see a couple trying to waltz by pulling each other round with the free leg bent at the knee and the free foot swinging at right angles! Concentrate on keeping your free foot close to your skating foot, even by placing it against the skating foot in a T-position just prior to the actual Three Turn – this will help a great deal in giving control and stopping you rotating too far. It is essential, too, that each partner stands perfectly upright. Any leaning forwards or backwards is to be avoided and every effort must be made to step from heel to heel when changing feet.

FOURTEEN STEP

This is a splendid dance, lively and full of fun. It makes good use of skating movements and techniques. It is skated to March music at 3/4 or 6/8 time at 56/58 bars per minute. It is a compulsory dance in the Third Class (Bronze) Ice Dance Test.

It is a very old dance, having been invented in Vienna by Franz Schöller in 1889 and was called the Schöller March or Ten-step. Later on it had four new steps added and became known as the Fourteenstep. To-day some skaters still call this dance the Ten-Step.

The dance is skated with a half-rink sequence. That is, two sequences are required for each circuit of the rink. It is known as a Set Pattern dance, that is the steps must be skated at specific points on the ice surface. The men's and ladies' steps are different. The dance is skated in the Waltz hold.

The dance commences with a run sequence, the man skating forward and the lady backwards aimed towards the barrier and then curving away from it. This is followed by a swing roll of four beats which curves the opposite way. The opening steps are then repeated followed by the man skating a Rfi open Mohawk at the same time the lady steps from Rbo to Lfo. For a moment the waltz hold changes to a foxtrot or open position on the 8th step. Following the Lbi edge the man skates a backward run sequence whilst the lady crosses her right foot behind the left on a forward inside edge, following this step with a run sequence and Lfo open Mohawk. Whilst the man skates Rbo followed by a cross-in-front Lbi after which he steps forward and the lady skates an Lbi, after which the sequence is repeated and the dance re-commences.

The dance required good posture on the swings and has quite steep edges. It requires good soft knee action and control of the partners' shoulders to check any over rotation on the turns.

The steps

Step No.	Man	Lady	Beats of music
		Description	
1	Lfo	Rbo	1
2	Rfi (Run)	Lbi (Run)	1
3	Lfo	Rbo	2
4	*Rfo Swing Roll	*Lbo Swing Roll	4
*This must not be kicked but swung from the hips			
5	Lfo	Rbo	1
6	Rfi (Run)	Lbi (Run)	1
7	Lfo	Rbo	2
8	Rfi (Open Mohawk)	Lfo (Step forward)	1
9	Lbi	Rfi (crossed behind)	1
10	Rbo	Lfo	1
11	Lbi (Run)	Rfi (Run)	1
12	Rbo	Lfo (Open Mohawk)	1
13	Lbi (crossed in front)	Rbo	1
14	Rfi (step forward)	Lbi	2
Repeat			

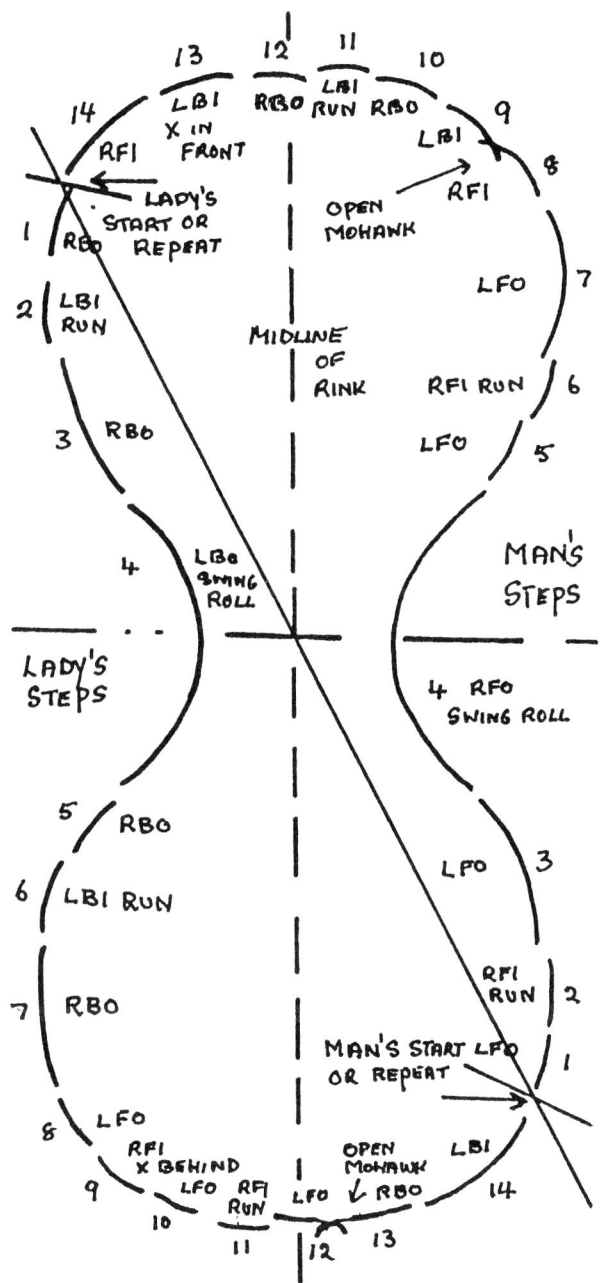

Set pattern and steps for the 'Fourteen Step' ice dance.

THE FIESTA TANGO

This is not commonly skated in Britain, which is a pity, because it is a very attractive dance. Both partners skate the same steps in the same forward direction. The author was introduced to it by an American ice skater. It makes use of the steps learned in the previous dances, including the Fourteen Step.

This is a nice dance making use of forward and backward edges, cross strokes, runs, a crossed-behind chassé, an open Mohawk and a swung change edge. It is skated in a Reverse Kilian position, that is, the man skates with the lady on his left side. During the dance (which contains 16 steps) there is a change of hold from Reverse Kilian to Kilian on steps 10 and 11, then back to Reverse Kilian again on step 16 when the partners step forward.

On step 8, which is a change edge swing roll, both free legs must swing together from a good bend of skating knee, rise, and bend of the knee. This edge counts 6-beats, and immediately after it is completed the lady moves slightly ahead of her partner on a left forward outside edge in preparation for the Open Mohawk turn on step 10.

If you and your partner are ambitious it is comparatively easy to learn the steps backwards as well, so that the dance becomes even more impressive. It is also a good basis for working into a free skating, or free dance programme, especially so if the swing change edge is executed with spirit.

This introduces the skater to dancing to Tango rhythm, which is a rhythm especially suitable for skating. It is danced in slower time than on the ballroom floor, but with proper rise and fall of the skating knee, a good tango effect can be obtained.

Steps of the Fiesta Tango

Step No.	Description	Beats of music
1	Lfo	2
2	Rfo	2
3	Lfo	1
4	Rfi Run	1
5	Lfo aimed at centre	2
6	Rfo Cross roll	2
7	Lfi Crossed behind chassé	2
8	Rfo-i Swing Roll	6

The swing of the free leg is from beat 3, the change of edge on beat 4, and the leg swings back. It is optional for the leg to remain in a forward position.

9	Lfo	2

Steps 10-11 partners change to Kilian hold.

10	Rfi Open Mohawk	1
11	Lbi	1

Step No.	Description	Beats of music
12	Rbo	2
13	Lbi	2
14	Rbo	2
15	Lbi Crossed in front	2
16	Rfi Partners change of Reversed Kilian hold	2

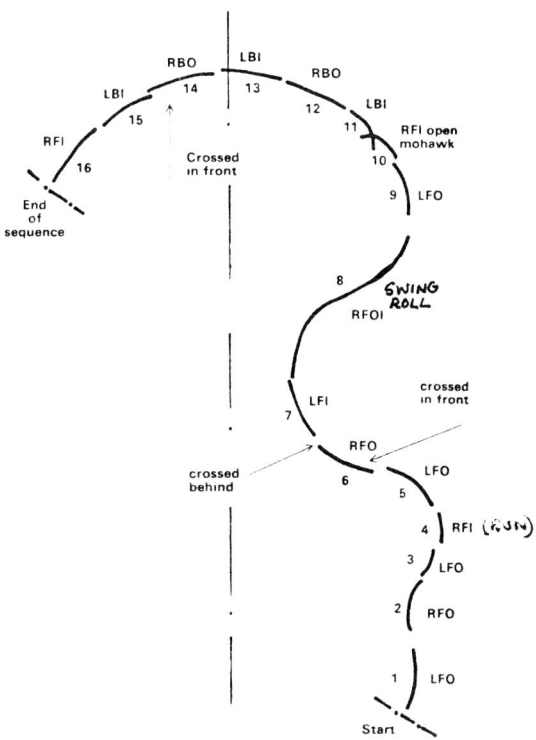

Steps and rink pattern for the Fiesta Tango.

9. Free Skating – Solo and Pairs

SOLO SKATING

Free Skating includes both solo skating and pair skating. If you have ambitions to turn professional and skate for a living, the choice may lie between (a) teaching and (b) show skating. There is a desperate shortage of male skaters at the moment for both fields, but the qualifications are different. Many champions and successful competition skaters turn to show skating first, because they feel it is a continuation of their free skating. Others turn professional in order to teach. In either event, a good ability to perform free skating and dancing is necessary. However, for the coach it is also important to have a good knowledge of school figures and compulsory dances, and many vacancies specify the necessary qualifications as Silver or Second Class standards at least. Show skaters fall into the categories of individual acts, stars or supporting acts, and line or chorus skaters. Individual acts may include free skating, pair skating, dancing, or comedy and 'knock-about' numbers. For the line or chorus skater, it is necessary to be able to skate figures reasonably well and be able to executive simple jumps, lifts, and so forth.

Not all skaters, however, wish to take proficiency tests, win competitions, or turn professional. They skate for the sheer enjoyment of it – and free skating, performed solo, is an exhilarating experience. Movements in free skating include dance steps, linking steps from movement to movement, jumps, spins, spirals, Spread Eagles, arabesques and so on, but all free skating is based, intrinsically, on proper edges and body positions.

SPIRALS AND ARABESQUES

Most skaters, when confronted with the word 'spiral' immediately try to skate over one foot with the body bent forwards from the waist and

An 'Arabesque' position skated on a spiral.

the free leg held very high behind, but this is only one form of spiral – the arabesque. A spiral is an edge, skated on one foot, with the body erect, at a good speed and held for the minimum of one circle. The term spiral is used because, if an edge is held continuously, the radius of the curve decreases gradually and you skate a curve that gets smaller as the speed drops.

As a rule, male skaters skate their arabesques and spirals in a more upright position than female skaters. The latter may even be able to skate bent so far forwards that their head is well below the skating knee, with the free leg held high, and in continuous line with the spin. When skating an arabesque, the back should be arched so that the free leg and the head are higher than the body. There is no set position for the arms during a spiral or arabesque, but the golden rule is never to let your back slump. Your free foot must always be turned out and your toe pointed gracefully. The secret is in stretching to the fullest extent.

At the beginning you will tend to skate too far forward on your skate when performing a forward spiral; your weight must be well back, otherwise there is a danger of catching your toe-pick and of falling unexpectedly and heavily.

JUMPS AND SPINS

The first basic in jumping is the ability to leave the surface of the ice. The actual turning and rotation are of secondary importance, so begin by jumping on both feet.

Skate forwards, bring both feet close together parallel to each other; now spring into the air from strongly bent knees. At the same time, lift your arms in front of you. You will jump a few inches into the air and, the moment you land, bend your knees and continue skating on both feet. Repeat this a few times until you are landing correctly over the skates, without your weight being tilted to either side.

Now, once again using the same take off, as you leave the rink surface, turn in the air to one side or another. You will describe a semi-circle and find yourself landing backwards. As you hit the ice, bend both knees and keep your feet parallel. Then extend your arms to the side. Try this until you are taking off and landing without wobbles or bending.

To jump from backwards to forwards; skate backwards, draw both feet close together and parallel again. Now, with body upright and head up, swing your arms to the front and spring upwards. *After you have sprung*, turn forwards. You will find that you turn easily in the air and will land on both skates, with knees well bent, in a forwards position. See that you land with your body in a perfectly upright position. You are now ready to tackle the simple jumps.

THE BUNNY HOP

This is a simple jump in which the skater travels straight forward. It is a useful movement to break the monotony of running steps and at the same time may increase the skater's speed over the ice. It may be performed as a solo movement or in unison with another skater in pair skating either apart or in the Kilian hold.

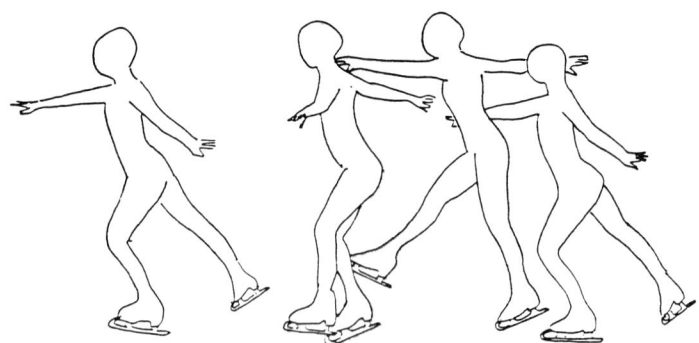

Bunny Hop Jump
Direction of skating – right to left ← A. Skate on left foot forward and jump B. Swing right foot forward. C. Land on right toe pick. D. Immediately skate on left foot forward.

The skater travelling forward on one foot springs off that foot and lands on the toe pick of the other from which one immediately pushes off straight on to the flat of the blade of the jumping foot. The sequence for jumping a Bunny Hop off the left foot would be:

Left foot, jump forward
Land on right toe pick and immediately push on to Left foot

The foot on to which one lands on the toe pick is swung forward as the jump is made and brought back to land on the toe. A useful preliminary exercise is to skate forward and swing the free leg forward then back, striking the ice with the toe of the free foot when it is alongside the skating foot.

You are required to skate Bunny Hop jumps in N.S.A. Elementary Grade Tests F7 in Free Skating and P7 in Pair Skating.

THE THREE JUMP

This is also called the Waltz Jump. A true Three Jump is executed on one foot only, taking off from the outside edge and landing on the inside edge of the same skate. The Waltz Jump, however, is skated from a forward outside edge on one foot, turning in the air and landing backwards on an outside edge on the other skate.

Skate forward two or three short edges, then draw your feet together to get the feel of the take-off you have been making, i.e. get your knees bent and your body erect. Do this a couple of times, then skate boldly on to an outside edge on your left foot, swing your free foot forward past the skating leg in a straight position as the jumping take-off point is reached and, at the same time, bring your right arm forward. The swinging forward of the leg and arm will assist in the 'lift'.

Now do not try to turn round to backwards! The lift-off is made as the free foot swings past the skating foot and the jump is made out of the circle, *not round it*.

As you land on to the right outside edge, bend your right knee strongly, and still keep an upright position of the body. Stop your shoulder from rotating by holding your left arm forward and your right arm back. This will prevent the edge on which you have landed from curling into a circle. Extend your left leg behind your right leg with the toe turned out.

Remember at all times to keep your body upright, the take-off and landing knees bent, and your head upright. *Do not try to turn until you have actually taken off in the jump.*

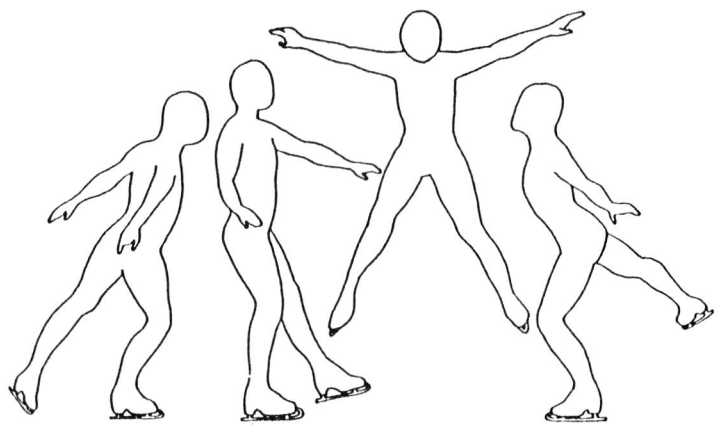

Sequence for Three (Waltz) Jump.
Direction of skating left to right. In this drawing the skater is taking the jump off the right foot in a clockwise rotation.

Once you can do this Three Jump, you have the basis of many other jumps. It is sound practice to skate a series of Three or Waltz Jumps in succession.

You have to do a Three Jump in Grade 8 Free Skating and Grade 7 in Pair Skating in the National Skating Association Elementary Grade Tests.

The Bunny Hop is a straight forward jump from one foot to the other and back again to the first foot without a turn in the air. The Three Jump is from forwards on one foot to backwards on the other with a half turn in the air. We now come to jumps which require one full turn.

THE TOE LOOP JUMP OR CHERRY FLIP

This is probably the easiest of the full turn jumps to learn. In this jump one goes from a backward edge on one foot to the same edge on the same foot, that is, one full turn. The jump is assisted by tapping the other foot with the toe pick into the ice.

The usual method to approach this jump is to skate forward on a left inside edge, the free foot is held to the front and the arms are open. Step on to a right forward inside edge. Let the free foot draw back and make an inside Three turn on to the back outside edge and then skate as nearly as possible straight. Keep the skating knee strongly bent and let the free leg extend to the rear. Now let the free foot cross the tracing and pick into

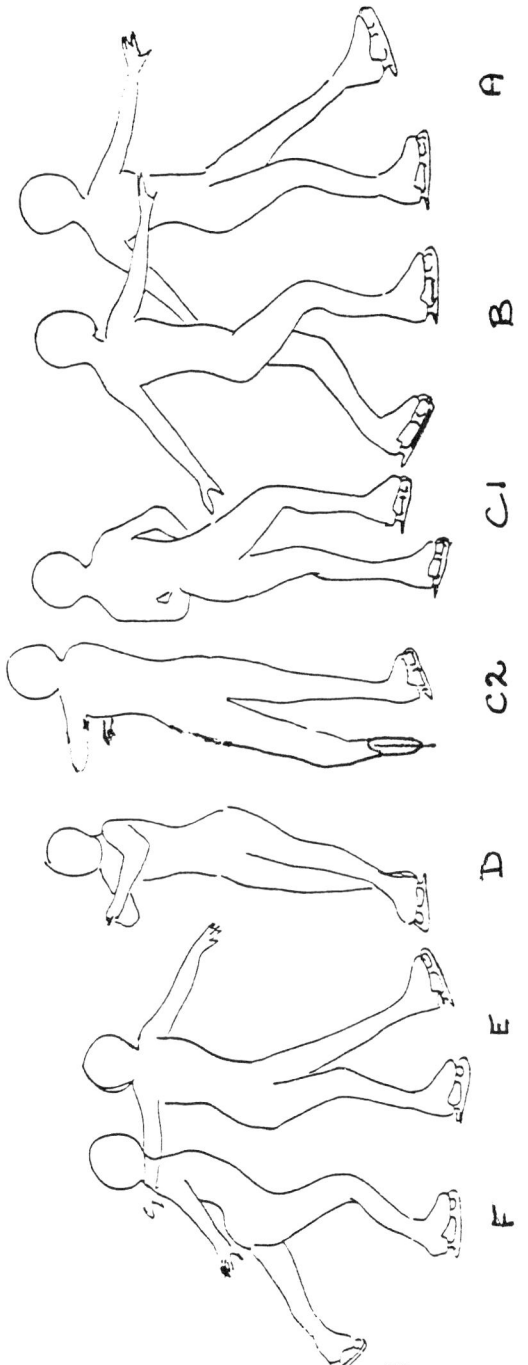

Sequence of Toe Loop or Cherry Flip Jump
Read the drawings right to left.
A   Commence on back outside edge.
B   Take free leg back.
C1 The toe pick of the free foot.
C2 hits the ice to lift off. Pull the arms in.
D   One full turn in the air with the feet crossed.
E   Land with free leg trailing.
F   Take free leg back, open the arms and keep a well bent skating knee on a back outside edge.

the ice about a foot on the inside. Drop the arms. Stretch both legs fully and using maximum lift use the arms to help and turn anti-clockwise and bring the arms together in front of your body. You may not believe it but at this position in the air your free leg is crossed! Just before landing the free leg is brought to the front and then immediately stretched to the rear. The landing is with a well bent knee with the head up and arms out. One often sees skaters attempting this jump from a position in which the free foot is not crossed but placed to one side of the skating foot and the skater turns forward and jumps off the toe pick of the free foot. This is bad practice and is not a Cherry Flip Jump at all. There should be hardly any pause throughout the jump from initial three turn to landing, the tap into the ice and the jump should be smooth and flowing.

THE SALCHOW JUMP

This jump gets its name from the famous skater who invented it. This involves a jump from an inside backward edge on one foot to a backward outside edge on the other, using a full turn in the air.

It is not very different from the Three Jump I have described earlier. The jump is made from an inside back edge and the landing is on an outside back edge. There are two ways of entering the jump. One may either skate a forward inside edge on, say, the right foot, then execute an Open Mohawk on to a left back inside edge. Or one may execute a left forward outside three on to a left back inside edge. The free leg is kept well back after the turn and must never come close up to the skating foot. Immediately after the three turn the swing is topped (there is no swing after a Mohawk turn entry), and the position of the back inside edge is held for some distance after which the free leg is thrown round to the front of the skating, take-off leg. This swinging round must not be violent. The rotation for the jump is obtained by steepening the back inside edge as the free leg is swung round. As the free foot crosses the tracing of the skating foot take off takes place by swinging the free leg outwards and upwards. The arms should assist in this lift. Landing is as described for the Toe Loop with open arms to check the turn and a strongly bent landing knee.

You will need to be able to execute a Salchow jump if you take the P9 Elementary Grade Test in Pair Skating.

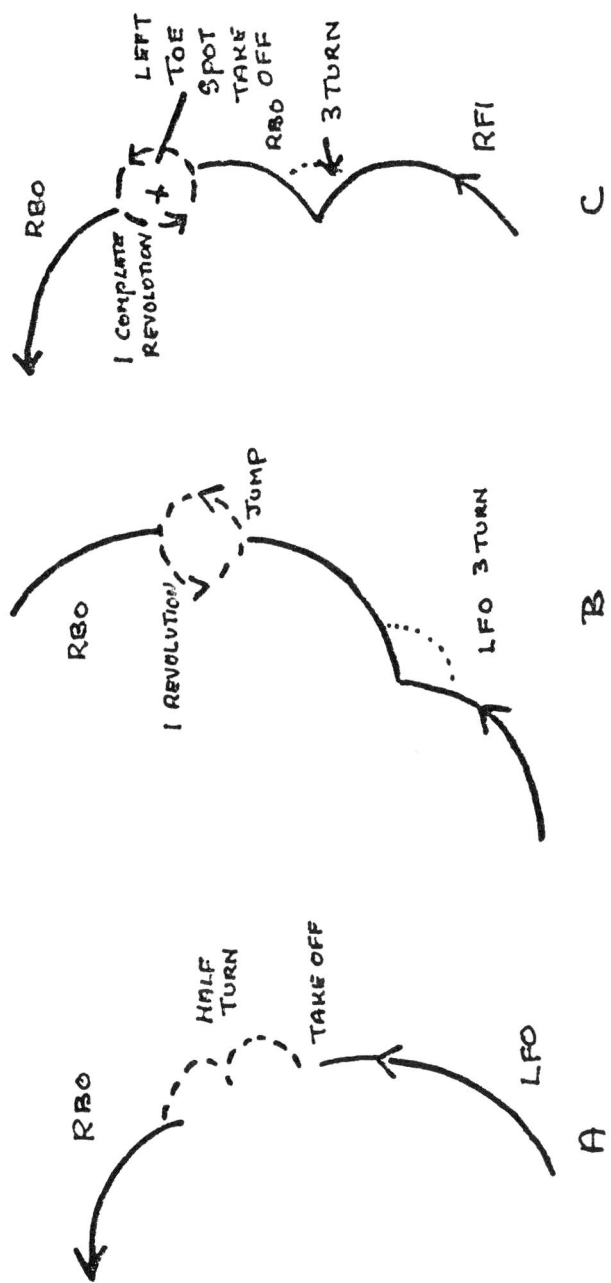

Tracings for (A) Three (Waltz) Jump, (B) Salchow Jump, (C) Toe Loop Jump (Cherry Flip).

SPINS AND PIROUETTES

Learning to spin is fun! The first problem is to learn to overcome the dizziness which follows the spin. However, in a remarkably short time you will get used to rotating and will be able to come out of even a long and fast spin without any giddiness or loss of direction. There are many different spins executed with the body in an upright position. They may be executed with the free leg leading or behind with partial use of the two picks or on the flat of the blade.

Let us start with a simple spin on one foot on the flat of the blade. First of all, get on to a forward outside edge (most skaters use the right foot) and turn a Three to inside back. Allow your left shoulder to come forwards and press your right shoulder back. Step forwards on to your left foot on an outside edge, bend your skating knee strongly, straighten it, turn a Three to back inside and allow your right shoulder to come forwards while pushing your left shoulder back. As you commence the rotation which follows, straighten your skating leg and push down hard on to the ball of your foot. Keep your arms equally to the side and front. As the spin begins, bring your free leg to the front and gradually draw your arms in. As the free leg is brought forward and the arms drawn in, the rotation will increase in speed. To come out of the spin, open your arms.

At first you will not actually spin, but will make a series of small circles which will gradually become even smaller and the spin will develop. The main difficulty of the spin is to 'centre' it, i.e. you must not travel off the original spot on which the spin started. The strong body rotation referred to will help you stay on the spot.

Once you have learned how to execute a spin on the flat of the blade, you can try the Scratch Spin, in which you rise on to the front part of the blade and use the two picks. To complete a Scratch Spin you bring your free leg forward over the front foot of your skating leg and lower your foot, so that your free ankle lies above the instep of your spinning foot. This gives great speed in the spin.

DANCE STEPS

These are linking steps used to keep the skater moving about the surface in a free skating programme and to connect the various movements, spins, jumps, etc. being executed.

Movements such as continuous changes of edge, Mohawks, spirals and arabesques, and Spread Eagles are used. Provided they are intelligently employed to enable the skater to cover the whole of the skating

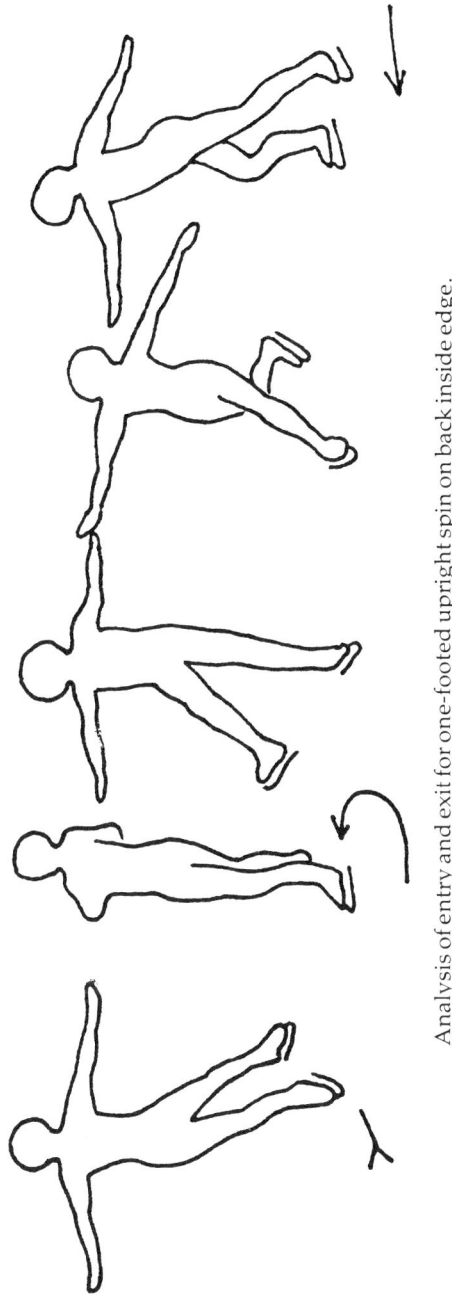

Analysis of entry and exit for one-footed upright spin on back inside edge.

area and balance the programme, the emphasis must be on originality and flexibility. It is very easy to copy the better skaters and acquire 'set' free skating steps. How much better to experiment and work out your own!

To begin with, the steps in the Fourteen Step used by the man have been referred to, and it needs little effort to build on them. For example, after the inside forward Mohawk, you can then turn round completely and step forward on to the left outside edge and execute a Three Turn, followed by an outside back on the right foot, a cross-over left back inside and step forwards to right forward inside, cross behind left forward inside and do an inside Mohawk to back right inside.

To free skate effectively, you must be proficient in skating on both feet and able (apart from spins and jumps) to execute movements forwards and backwards, to right and left.

Pair skaters in particular need to practise running together and to execute steps and movements both in holds and in 'shadow', i.e. not touching. It is helpful to practise skating school figures together, jumping together to get the timing of take-off and landing right, and spinning apart. Good pair skating requires the constant supervision of a very experienced coach and this should be sought at the outset.

There are a number of movements (other than the ones already mentioned) which can help to express the music and to carry the skater in full coverage of the rink surface. Typical of such movements are the Teapot, the Drag, and the Spread Eagle.

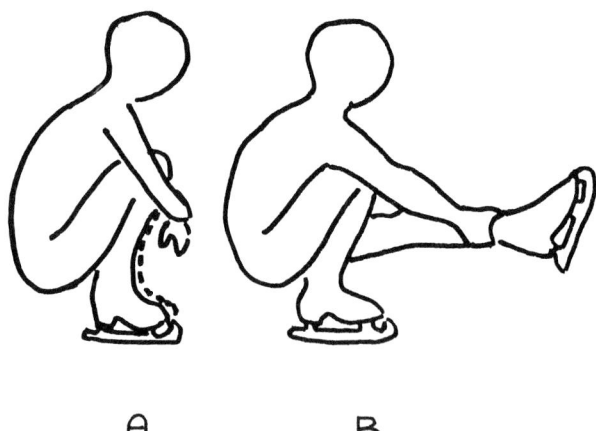

A   B

The Tea Pot (this is also the Sit Spin position).
A. Preparatory position on both feet.
B. Position on one foot with free leg extended.

THE TEAPOT

The Teapot is very popular with younger skaters and affords excellent training for the Sit Spin later. To skate a Teapot, get up a good speed skating forwards, then bend your skating knee and lower yourself so that you are in a squatting position. At the same time, bend your body forwards from the hips and extend your free foot straight forwards past your skating foot. This movement has the advantage that, if you should fall off it, you simply sit down on the rink. When you have mastered the forward Teapot, it is exciting, and equally easy, to try a backwards Teapot.

THE DRAG

This is a pretty movement in which you skate forward on one foot, then bend your skating knee fully, but keep your body perfectly erect and square to the tracing. At the same time, swing your free leg back and place the inside of your skating foot on the rink and drag it behind you. This is a nice movement particularly for pair skaters, but, a word of caution – it can put undue wear on the side of your boot, so it must not be done too frequently. White boots are particularly prone to suffer in this way.

The 'Drag' position.

THE SPREAD EAGLE

This is a movement in which both feet are on the rink at the same time, with the heels inwards and the toes turned away from each other. You should stand perfectly erect with your legs fully extended with straight

Spread Eagle.

knees. The inside Spread Eagle, skated on inside edges, is the easiest of the movements, but the Spread Eagle may be skated on an outside edge, requiring more courage, or in a straight line. Make sure that your bottom is not sticking out when you do this and that your head is carried high.

These three free skating movements should be practised on both feet. They can be used to link other steps together, and even to commence or finish any programme.

One compulsory figure which can be introduced into free skating is the use of the change of edge. Whether skated to lead into a turn or jump, or used in spiral form to cover the whole rink, the change edge is an attractive movement to watch and is, moreover, one of the figures which a skater can really 'feel' when performing. The actual feel of a change of edge at high speed in an arabesque cannot properly be described – it has to be experienced – but it epitomises the freedom of skating in a personal way.

FREE SKATING PROGRAMMES

I think that the real joy and fun of skating lies in free skating executed as a programme. One can either piece together various steps and movements to skate to music on an ad lib basis, enjoying the music and letting it lead you from movement to movement or one can carefully

Two movements which may be skated in a free skating programme. (*Left*) A teapot skated backwards at a good speed is spectacular. (*Right*) A simple two-footed jump (without turning in the air) can be an attractive linking movement in a free skating programme.

work out a programme to selected music, so that they become a harmonious whole.

When I refer to free skating I am also including pair skating and free dancing within the term, though this is not strictly correct. It is great fun to vary dance steps to suit music, and even pair skating can be done on an ad hoc basis.

Once your can *skate* edges, do simple jumps and spins, and perform simple linking steps and dance steps, *in good form*, a free skating programme becomes possible. Free skating is not only good fun for the skater, if the movements are executed surely and in good style, however simple, but it also provides pleasure for spectators.

Initially the coach prepares the first free skating programme for a pupil, to show how to place the movements on the ice, how to spread out and balance the various elements, and how to select and skate to music. After that, however, you should not rely solely upon your teacher: you must use your own imagination to make up the programme, but always be ready to accept or seek guidance on technical matters, on presentation, and on matters which require experience. In fact, the budding free skater must learn to be his or her own choreographer!

Many clubs and associations hold primary competitions for novices and young skaters, and quite often the free skating competitions are limited to a jump, a spiral and a spin, and a programme length not exceeding 1½ minutes duration. It is customary, too, in such competitions for only the very simple jumps and spins to be performed or allowed, and advanced steps, jumps, etc. are excluded, and can even penalize the skater!

The first step is to consider what you *can* do. Never try to include in a programme any movement or turn in which you are not proficient and confident. Having decided the movements you wish to use, the worst thing is to go out on the ice and try to put these into a programme immediately! Skate the movements individually. Try to skate at the speed you will be skating in the competition or exhibition and ascertain just how much surface each movement will cover. Having selected your music, which should not be too hackneyed or too trendy, skate some of your movements to the music and find out how many bars each move takes. Then get off the ice and start on the clerical work!

Make a map of the rink, marking on the centre line and transverse axes (as in the dance diagram layout), and place the movements on paper where you think they will take place. In this way it becomes easy to visualize the presentation and to plan the movements so that there is a balance. One cannot see oneself skating, unless a video-tape or ciné film is made, or a large mirror available.

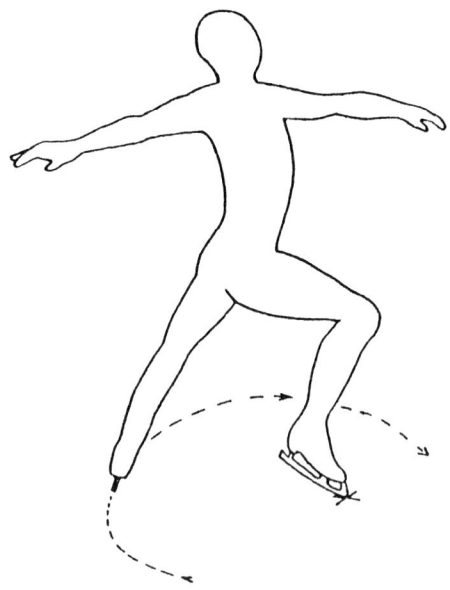

The Forward Pivot.

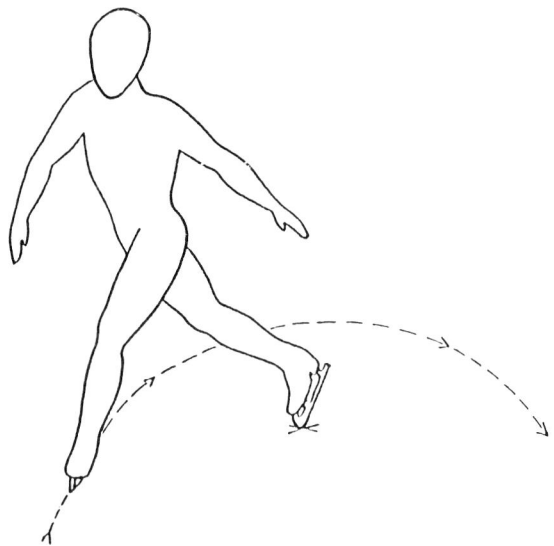

The Back Pivot.

Remember, you must not skate in one direction round the rink all the time, or place jumps and spins in a far corner. Nor should you execute all your best jumps and spins all together. Try to remember that in a competition the judges will be placed along one side of the rink and that, if you skate intricate or spectacular movements close to the judges' side and in a corner at the same time, it is hardly likely that they will be able to see them properly or mark them to greatest advantage. Try to place your spins along the centre line of the rink, and your best jumps across the centre spot. Above all, there must be continuous practice and rehearsal, until the whole programme becomes automatic and yet still looks alive and spontaneous. Should you fall or stumble, you can then get up and carry on skating as if nothing had happened. There is nothing worse than a slight fault which ends in a skater wandering about the rink trying to remember what step to do next and suffering from a brief loss of memory.

Start nicely, to attract attention, and then gradually skate with a continually improving programme until your best and most spectacular movements enable you to finish in such a way that judges and spectators would like to see more, and even feel that the programme was short. A boring, inefficient skater can make a two-minute programme seem like half an hour to the audience.

Before starting a programme, it is customary to have what is termed a warming up period on the ice, to skate around, loosen your muscles, and relax a little. Don't overdo this, Practise a few simple movements, get used to the ice, and quit before you either get tired or find yourself missing a difficult movement. Let the other competitors or exhibitors do that – it is the easiest thing in the world to leave the winner's place on the warming-up ice.

No matter how many times a skater performs or skates in a competition, the period before skating out on the ice is one when nerves are going to be tested. Your stomach will feel queer, your throat and mouth dry . . . but, the moment you skate out to take up your starting pose and the familiar music commences, all your nervousness will vanish and you will be able to concentrate on the task in hand.

PAIR SKATING

This is regarded by experienced skaters as the most difficult yet the most beautiful form of skating. A pair consists of a man and lady, or boy and girl, and finding a partner for pair skating isn't easy!

Pair skating is free skating, there are no compulsory figures in pair skating tests or competitions. There is, however, in pair skating a short programme in which certain elements have to be skated, followed by a free programme.

In pair skating the emphasis is on 'unison', and a couple must really move as one. Alignment of legs, arms, bodies must be simultaneous and exact. Lean and sway of bodies must exactly match, and every movement must be 'together'. The impression given by pair skaters must be of unison and harmonious composition. Though they need not always perform the same movements, and may separate from time to time, joining up and separations must be in complete accord.

Finding a partner

Size is very important and the girl must be slightly smaller than the boy. This is necessary because it not only looks better but makes it easier for the boy to lift his partner. However, there must not be too great a difference in size otherwise the partnership can look unbalanced, even ridiculous. Next, the technical ability of the partners must be similar though it is better if the boy is a slightly better skater than the girl. The boy must be strong enough to be able to lift his partner and if the girl is too heavy at the beginning it is obvious that there will be no future for that partnership!

If the couple are very young the possibility of the girl outgrowing the boy must also be thought of – because this may be a very sorry end for a

These photographs show four free skating movements which may be used in a single or pair skating programme.
(*Top left*) An arabesque skated on a spiral.
(*Top right*) An outside edge Spread Eagle.
(*Bottom left*) An exciting moment, the entry by a young pair into the 'Death Spiral'. The boy is about to get into a back pivot: note how the girl has her free foot crossed over her skating foot.
(*Bottom right*) A pose indicating the end of a programme.

partnership which has worked together and begun to achieve a skating reputation.

Finally, the next question to be settled is: how are the two going to get on together off the ice?

Pair skating takes longer to achieve than individual skating – and patience and continual rehearsals are vital ingredients. There are two types of pair skating. In one type the couple are in 'holds' and skate together: in the other type they may skate identical movements separated, this is called 'shadow skating'. If they skate opposite movements whilst separated this is called 'mirror skating'.

First Pair steps

These require as much time off the ice as on the ice! First of all practice skating round the rink together in the Kilian hold. Practise skating both clockwise and anti-clockwise, and then in a large figure of eight, crossing the rink at the transverse axis. Then practise the same movements with an extended arm hold. All the time make certain that the hold is firm and that pushing off on the stroke is well timed, the rise and fall, bending and straightening of the skating knees match perfectly. The free legs must be extended properly, neither higher than the other, and the free feet turned out gracefully. Don't forget the feet follow the knee so if the knee is turned out the feet will follow naturally!

Stopping and starting together must be rehearsed over and over again until it is just like one person performing. Then practise all these movements again in the Reverse Kilian hold. Head and shoulders should work in unison and the head held upright. It is sound practice to skate school figures, edges and eights, tracing the circles, turning the threes and rockers. Synchronised footwork is essential.

Shadow skating

The boy and girl must skate in unison doing the same movements, edges and turns, without holding each other, so that one appears to be the other's shadow! Speed must match, and again great care must be taken to see that changes of step correspond exactly.

When you have succeeded in these movements the pair should skate in the Waltz Hold. It is harder to coordinate the footwork skating in this hold, but again use of backward and forward edges and runs must be practised. It is not always necessary to use the full ice surface. Pair movements should be practised in a small area, to make certain they are right. They should also be practised off the ice so that they become natural to them both.

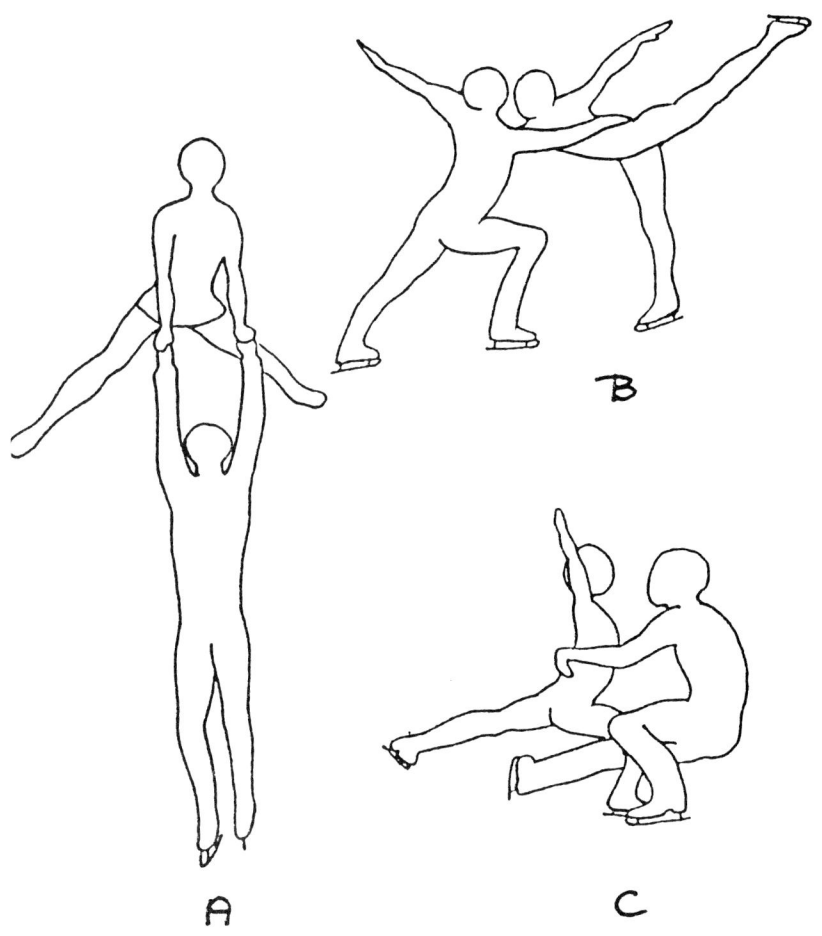

A. Pair skating can be dangerous.
B. Pair skating can be beautiful.
C. Typical pair spin.

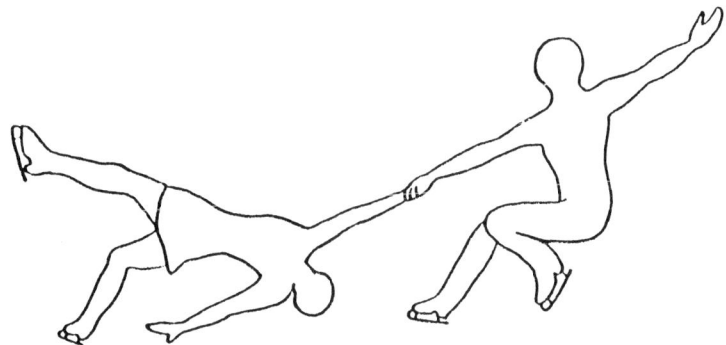

The pair skating 'Death Spiral'.

Spins and Lifts

Pairs spin in holds or separately. Great care must be taken to ensure that whilst both enter the spin at the same time, if doing synchronised separate spins, they must take the same number of rotations and emerge from the spin simultaneously.

Lifts are an essential part of pair skating. The pair must use firm straight arms to support the lift. The girl must spring from a strongly bent knee a fraction of a second *before* the man starts to lift her. The man uses his strength fractionally *after* the lady has started her jump into the lift. This ensures that the whole movement becomes smooth and not just a feat of muscular strength.

Periodically the pair must 'walk through' their programme or sections of it and give even the smallest details the greatest attention. It is the job of the man partner to show off or display his partner, and because either partner will make mistakes from time to time, each has to learn how to give and take and co-operate.

First programmes will consist of running together, spirals and arabesques, dance steps, simple jumps, lifts, and spins. UNTIL THESE ARE PERFECTED AND SKATED IN HARMONY AND UNISON THERE CAN BE NO PROGRESS ON TO MORE DIFFICULT MOVEMENTS – remember medals, tests and championships are won by the couples who perfect these basic techniques.

In the assisted Waltz Jump in the NSA Pair Badge test the couple start in waltz hold. The man skates forward, the lady backward to enter this movement. The man then turns a forward outside three to backward inside edge, then changes to back outside edge on the other foot, whilst she turns from backward edge to forward. When she is ready to spring she lowers her right arm so that the man's left hand is low, then keeping that arm perfectly straight, he lifts his right hand so that it fits into her left armpit. As she springs from a forward outside edge (as in the solo Three Jump) he straightens the arm under her armpit and both keep the other arm straight. She is thus lifted easily into the air. As she does a half turn in the air the man does a half turn on the ice.

A word of caution. Lifts and jumps can be very dangerous and you should only practise them under the watchful eye of a teacher, but you can put in plenty of practise on these movements off the ice, which makes it easier when you come to do them with skates on.

In separate movements you must pace yourselves in order to get back together at the right moment, and if this doesn't happen the whole effect of the programme is lost.

Plenty of practice, and more practice, and even more practice is necessary to achieve pair skating, but it has its reward in being the most beautiful of skating disciplines.

Pairs must be in unison.

10. Outdoor Ice Skating

Outdoor ice skating falls into two types: artificial rinks out-of-door and natural ice formations. The latter includes lakes, reservoirs, ponds, rivers, canals and so on. The former category consists of proper outdoor rinks (sometimes with refrigerating equipment as in indoor rinks) and artificial rinks caused by the temporary flooding of fields, arenas etc. specifically for skating.

Outdoor skating, especially over natural ice, is a wonderful sport, particularly when one skates a long distance on canals or frozen rivers, or over large lakes. The air is clean, fresh and invigorating, and the ice surface, when at its best, 'sings' as one swoops along. On the other hand, skating, figures in particular, on an outdoor rink or over a frozen pond can pose problems. Firstly, there is the wind to consider: going one way round a figure can be fine, but the return journey against the wind, or with the wind, can wreck a tracing completely. Secondly, the ice surface can vary. On an indoor rink the ice is resurfaced between sessions, and on artificial outdoor rinks, this, too, is carried out, but over ponds and lakes the surface will vary according to the freezing conditions. The ice may be corrugated from wind action, branches or flotsam may be frozen into the surface to bring hazards to the skater, whilst the quality of the ice may vary. This can bring dangers if one should meet patches of thin or rotten ice, especially at the beginning of a freeze-up or after a thaw has started. Good outdoor ice is superb, however. It is even better than the artificial variety, and skating over this ice is the most exhilarating and thrilling experience for any ice skater!

Large expanses of ice which have only a few inches of water beneath or which is very thick due to an extreme climate are probably quite safe for racing and speed events, ice hockey and general skating. Cracks in the ice do not necessarily mean that it is dangerous, though a covering of an inch or so of snow may be: you may hit unseen obstacles such as sticks or stones, or run on to dangerous ice.

Clear black or green ice is stronger than white ice or snow ice. In general, for safety's sake, a minimum of two inches of black ice of five inches of snow ice is recommended. Always remember that for any type of ice its thickness is no real gauge of its safety.

Do *not* use your best skates for outdoor work over natural ice. The different conditions – hard and soft ice, corrugations or material frozen into the surface – can soon take the edge off your skates. It is best, too, to take the toe-picks from the front or grind them down, so that the grounded front of your skate will ride over obstacles instead of bringing you down. A typical hazard occurs when ice cracks and one piece rides higher than the other, and then freezes. The step thus formed, even if it is a small one, can cause a nasty tumble.

Remember, too, to wear warm clothes and take some extra ones to put on when you stop skating. If you are skating school figures you may well need to wear a pair of gloves. You should also take some extra clothes just in case you go through the ice.

If you fall through ice into deep water, you will be in very real danger of drowning, let alone freezing to death. If you go through when you are travelling at speed, you will be thrown forward, away from the hole, under the ice. Assuming that the shock of icy waters does not immobilize you and that you can swim, you must try to find the hole that you made, which from under the surface shows up as a light patch against the dark ice.

If you see someone else go through the ice, try to find a long pole or rope to help him or her out, and do not let too many other people go near the hole. When the ice is quite thin and the water fairly shallow, say only a couple of feet, there is less difficulty, providing of course that it is not a small child who has fallen through: you can usually break a way through the ice to give assistance.

The wisest thing to do, if you are going to skate on natural ice, is to learn first of all how to swim. This may not only save your own life but might also prevent someone else losing his life trying to save you; you may, in addition, be called upon to save a friend.

Skating outdoors on natural ice is where the sport began; its magic is still strong and, no doubt, always will be.

11. Now You Can Ice Skate...

Once a skater has become fairly proficient at moving about in different steps and simple dances, the confines of the public session tend to become irksome: more space is needed, skaters of all degrees of proficiency are struggling to get a fair share of the rink, and it is difficult trying to practise. True, there are the dance intervals during which you may try your skill with either a professional or an amateur partner, but these do not satisfy the needs of the figure and free skater.

The solution lies, in many instances, in club facilities. Most rinks have an amateur skating club attached, affiliated to the national organization, where there are sessions for learning steps and dances, and where junior club, inter-club, and senior competitions are held. Such clubs are always ready to welcome the keen skater, but not so willing to welcome older social skaters. Clubs, too, generally require the candidate for membership to be able to skate some form of entrance test. Clubs do bring skaters together and provide a rare opportunity for the champion to skate with the learner. Some clubs unfortunately are beset by a 'win at all costs' attitude and certain of their members, instead of helping the less proficient, are merely there to use the club sessions as practice sessions and to collect all the trophies they can. A good club, on the other hand, will provide invaluable help.

It is absolutely essential for the beginner to have professional coaching as soon as possible. This book is intended to put the skater on the right lines and help him or her to skate properly, but private professional tuition is essential if progress is to be maintained. Select your instructor – for the male dancer a female teacher and a male teacher for the female pupil does make it easier. *For pairs, a good teacher is essential from the start.* For the figure skater, use of the rink between sessions, on what are termed 'patches', under the watchful eye of a coach is vital.

But, a word of caution: too many teachers are obsessed with getting as many pupils as possible to pass proficiency tests. This is good for national associations, as test fees are their life blood, but, in the end, this means the loss of many keen skaters annually. Though the number of skaters is enormous, the number who actually take proficiency tests and become members of national associations is quite small, and expands at an extremely slow rate. So, try to find an instructor who will encourage you to learn new movements, as well as one who will give sound basic training.

For the skater who wants to win titles, it is a long hard slog. You need endless practice time. Your skating is going to cost a great deal of money and you are going to have to eat, sleep and drink skating and skating techniques for 25 hours out of every 24! It is a sad and indisputable fact that an amateur devotes most of his or her time to practising and quite often, for years, has no regular or full-time employment whilst learning and practising. Indeed, the top amateur skaters of today are dedicated individuals who know little of anything else and are virtually 'professionals' insofar as skating time and opportunity are concerned.

Skating profiency tests, though they are introduced with a view to encouraging the newcomer and to increasing the efficiency of techniques, unfortunately become harder each season. The standard gradually rises: one has only to see youngsters today quickly picking up techniques such as double jumps which a few years ago was unheard of. So, as you become more proficient, we ask you to give a helping hand to other, less competent skaters. Skate dances with a youngster or an older enthusiast and do not be afraid to give a helping hand (providing the professional coach who might be involved does not object). Be prepared to join in activities which will improve not only your own skating, but those of other people. Today there is unfortunately a sort of 'Hate-the-Hun' attitude in certain competitive quarters – please do not indulge in this. Skating gives you an opportunity to enjoy your sport with your family, with friends, with old and young enthusiasts, with people of other nationalities and from other clubs.

If you aim to take proficiency tests, work hard at them and truly to be a credit to your coach. Attend the test properly and neatly dressed, having checked your skates some days beforehand, with clean skating boots, and with a ready, cheerful smile. If the judges' decision goes against you, try to be cheerful about it and do not mutter about 'unfair judges', 'poor skating surface', 'bad music', 'rotten partner', 'poor coach', or whatever other comments one has heard skaters make in the past. You are not perfect and, though you and your coach may have felt you deserved to pass, the judges probably saw something your coach had missed or mistakes you made in the stress of the test.

Ice skating is a terrific sport, it is artistic and it can open horizons to you for years to come. Skaters who give up the sport generally return to it in later years, and some go on until they are well and truly in the octogenarian class! So, on with your ice skates and get out on that ice to glide, spin, jump, dance, swerve and swoop!

Sequence photographs of an Axel Paulsen jump. This difficult jump is taken off from a forward outside edge on one foot, with 1½ turns in the air before landing on the back outside edge of the other foot. The little girl in the photograph is only 9 years old. (Direction of jump →.)

Perfection! This skater demonstrates the beauty and artistry of an arabesque. The readers who thoroughly master the basic elements in this book should achieve the same balance and grace throughout all their skating movements.

THE NATIONAL SKATING ASSOCIATION

The National Skating Association of Great Britain, founded in 1879, is the controlling body for amateur figure, dance and speed skating on ice and rollers in the United Kingdom, and is recognised as such by the International Skating Union and the Fédération Internationale de Roller Skating. The N.S.A. promotes the organisation of skating tests, competitions, and championships in this country, and is responsible for the selection of candidates for training in the Government assisted coaching scheme. Championships in Scotland are organised by the Scottish Ice Figure Skating Association (who also have their own tests) and the Scottish-Speed-Skating union; both bodies are affiliated to the N.S.A).

The N.S.A. is also responsible for the selection of individual British skaters and teams to take part in international competitions, the European and World Championships, and the Olympic Winter Games.

12. N.S.A. Elementary Tests in Ice Skating

INTRODUCTION

The Elementary Tests were introduced in 1970 to provide an incentive for skaters of an elementary standard to progress systematically to higher levels of proficiency. The organisation of this group of tests is kept as informal and simple as possible, and candidates are not required to be members of the Association. An Elementary Test Record Card is held by the skater. This card is signed by the Judge after a successful test. The skater is then entitled to buy the appropriate cloth badge and may then proceed to the next grade of test.

The first group of six tests cover a range of skating techniques from being able to skate forwards and stop for Grade 1, through backwards skating and simple edges, to a change of edge movement and a Mohawk in Grade 6.

Nine additional tests of a higher elementary standard were introduced in June 1972. These are in three groups relating to Dance, Free and Pair Skating. At this stage, it is necessary for the candidates to skate more advanced movements and step sequences in good style.

Candidates for the Elementary Tests D7 to D9 in Ice Dancing are required to perform many of the step sequences and turns of the dances, skated as separate movements and without a partner, some of the movements must be executed to a specified rhythm although not to music.

The Tests F7 to F9 in Free Skating include step sequences, spirals, simple jumps and spins of a few revolutions. At this stage, the skaters are not required to skate a programme.

Candidates in Tests P7 to P9 in Pair Skating are judged as a pair consisting of lady and gentleman (of any age), both of whom must be amateurs. The pair skating movements consist of step sequences performed side by side, assisted jumps, simple lifts, pair spins and solo movements performed in unison. No music is required, but the skaters are expected to move in a well co-ordinated manner.

The Elementary Tests have proved to be extremely popular with the younger skaters. Since their introduction, some thousands of tests have been passed each year.

GENERAL REGULATIONS

Elementary Tests consist of the elementary skating movements which form the basis of Ice Dancing, Figure and Pair Skating.

The candidate need not be a member of the N.S.A. or of any Affiliated Club.

There is no fee for attempting the test, but the candidate is not entitled to take the next higher test until the badge for the test passed has been purchased.

The tests may be taken in a general skating session.

The first six tests must be taken progressively from 1 to 6.

There are three further tests in each of the following three branches of Ice Skating for which an additional Test Record Card will be issued:

> Dancing: D7, D8 and D9
> Free Skating: F7, F8 and F9
> Pair Skating: P7, P8 and P9

A candidate for these further tests must have passed Grades 1 to 6 of the Elementary Tests and may proceed through any branch (or branches), but in any branch, the tests must be taken progressively, 7 to 9.

A Test Record Card bearing the candidate's name will be issued at the rink prior to the candidate attempting the first grade of test. This card must be carefully retained by the candidate and presented for each subsequent test. On completion of a successful test, the Judge shall sign the appropriate section of the card. The candidate is entitled to purchase an N.S.A. badge for the test only on production of the Record Card, which shall then be countersigned by the person who issues the badge.

NATIONAL SKATING ASSOCIATION OF GREAT BRITAIN		
ELEMENTARY TEST RECORD		
TEST	DATE	JUDGES' SIGNATURE
GRADE ONE		
GRADE TWO		
GRADE THREE		
GRADE FOUR		
GRADE FIVE		
GRADE SIX		

Do not lose this card. It is the only record of your progress.

NSA Elementary Test Record Card for Grades 1-6. A separate card is issued for Grades 7-9 Elementary Tests. The skater who passes these Grades must carefully look after the card because it is the only record of his or her proficiency.

EXPLANATORY NOTES

Style

Good style should be aimed at throughout all tests. Generally an upright posture should be maintained, with the head erect. The arms should be sightly flexed and extended from the body sufficiently to obtain a pleasing position, with the hands carried at about waist level and the palms facing the ice surface with the fingers neither clenched not unduly spread. A flexible skating knee should be maintained on all applicable occasions with a moderately straight free leg.

Footwork

In skating strokes, neat footwork is to be maintained, which means bringing the feet level and closely together between the thrusts. The thrust is to be made from the side of the blade without the use of the toe point.

Edges

All edges skated consecutively, progressive sequences, etc., should be on curves which form part of a circle. Where applicable, the curves should be of approximately equal length.

Starting and Repetitions

The movements need not be started from rest and they may be skated across or along the rink as required by the judge. Sufficient steps should be skated to show the candidate's ability to perform the movement required. A fall does not, in itself, necessarily cause failure. A judge may require any movement to be re-skated.

Abbreviations

R = right	F = forward	O = outside
L = left	B = backwards	I = inside

TEST SCHEDULES

Elementary Tests — Grades 1 to 6

The first six tests are graded progressively from 1 to 6, and each movement of these tests must be skated solo.

Grade 1
(a) Forward skating on alternative feet.
(b) Forward stop (Snowplough, one foot Snowplough, Hockey or T Stop).

Grade 2
(a) Forward skating strokes on alternate feet, showing an understanding of use of blade, neat footwork and knee bend.
(b) Backward skating on alternate feet.

Grade 3
(a) Forward skating on alternate feet. Curves to be on outside edges.
(b) Gliding forward on one foot, R and L.
(c) Backward skating on alternate feet, showing an understanding of push-off and free foot position.

Grade 4
(a) Backward curves on alternate feet. Curves to be on outside edges of moderate length.
(b) Gliding backward on one foot, R and L.
(c) Step from backward to forward, R and L.

Grade 5
(a) Consecutive forward outside edges. Each edge to be about one-third of a circle.
(b) Consecutive forward inside edges. Each edge to about one-third of a circle.
(c) Continuous forward crossovers clockwise and counter-clockwise.
(d) Forward Outside Three turn, R and L, the edges before and after the turn being of approximately equal length.

Grade 6
(a) Continuous back crossovers, clockwise and counter-clockwise.
(b) Consecutive backward outside edges. Each edge to about one-third of a circle.
(c) Change of edge, forward outside to forward inside, R and L.
(d) Forward Mohawk, R and L, the edges before and after the turn being of about equal length.

Elementary Tests – Grades D7 to D9 in Ice Dancing

These tests are skated without a partner, and no music is required.

Although the tests are not skated to music, a rhythmic relationship is required between the steps in certain sequences, as an introduction to dancing to music. The time relationship of these step sequences is, therefore, given in terms of beats.

Introductory steps are optional, but should be kept to a minimum number not exceeding five.

Good style and neat footwork, as stipulated in the Explanatory Notes, must be maintained throughout this further group of tests.

Grade D7   (a) Forward open chassés repeated on alternate feet. (Lfo, chassé Rfi, Lfo – Rfo, chassé Lfi, Rfo, etc.). Timing 1, 1, 2 – 1, 1, 2, etc.

(b) Forward progressive (or run) sequence followed by an outside edge on which the free foot is swung slowly forwards, repeated on alternate feet. (Lfo, run Rfi, Lfo swing – Rfo, run Lfi, Rfo swing, etc.) Timing 1, 1, 4 – 1, 1, 4, etc.

(c) Forward outside Open Mohawk, R and L. The edges before and after the turn to be controlled and of about equal length.

(d) Forward outside three turn followed by back outside edge, R and L. (Fo three turn Bi, Bo). Timing 2, 1, 3. After the three turn, the free foot is to be placed on the ice close to the skating foot.

Grade D8   (a) Consecutive forward cross rolls, each edge to be about one-third of a circle.

(b) Backward open chassés, repeated on alternate feet. (Lbo chassé Rbi, Lbo – Rbo, chassé Lbi, Rbo, etc.). Timing 1, 1, 2 – 1, 1, 2, etc.

(c) Forward outside Closed Mohawk, R and L. The edges before and after the turn to be of about equal length.

(d) Forward outside Open Choctaw, R and L. The edges before and after the turn to be of about equal length.

Grade D9   (a) Consecutive backward cross rolls, each edge to be about one-third of a circle.

(b) Backward progressive (or run) sequence followed by an outside edge on which the free foot is swung slowly backwards, repeated on alternate feet. (Lbo, run Rbi, Lbo swing – Rbo, run Lbi, Rbo (swing, etc.). Timing 1, 1, 4 – 1, 1, 4, etc.

(c) Forward inside Closed Choctaw, R and L. The edges before and after the turn to be of about equal length.
(d) Forward step sequence; run, chassé, run: R and L. (Fo, run Fi, Fo, chassé Fi, Fo, run Fi, Fo). All edges to be of about equal length.

Elementary Tests – Grades F7 to F9 in Free Skating

These tests are skated solo and no music is required. Good style and neat footwork as stipulated in the Explanatory Notes must be maintained through all movements.

Introductory steps up to seven in number are optional.

Grade F7
(a) Forward Teapot or Drag on either foot.
(b) Run and Bunny Hop on either foot.
(c) Forward outside parallel spiral, either foot.
(d) Back outside pivot, either foot, at least one revolution.

Grade F8
(a) Forward inside parallel spiral, either foot.
(b) Three jump on either foot.
(c) Upright one-foot spin, at least three revolutions.
(d) Sequence of – inside Mohawk – back outside edge – step forward, at reasonable pace, R and L. (All edges of about equal length).

Grade F9
(a) Back outside parallel spiral, either foot.
(b) *Toe-Loop jump (Cherry Flip)*, on either foot.
(c) One-foot flat foot spin, at least three revolutions, with entry and exit movements on running edge.
(d) Six step sequence – Lfi – Mohawk to Rbi – Lbo – Rbo – cross in front Lbi – to step forward Rfi. (All edges of about equal length).

Elementary Tests – Grades P7 to P9 in Pair Skating

These tests are skated and judged as a pair, consisting of a lady and gentleman, both amateurs. A candidate may skate the test with a partner who has already passed the test.

No music is required. Good style and neat footwork as stipulated in the Explanatory Notes must be maintained through all movements.

Introductory steps up to seven in number are optional. Spins in all these tests should be at least three turns.

Grade P7
(a) Hand-in-hand forward runs, clockwise and counter-clockwise, lady may be on either side.

(b) Side-by-side (Kilian or Reverse Kilian hold), Bunny Hops, followed by forward parallel spiral.
(c) *Assisted* three jump for lady, in waltz position, but with the man's right hand under the lady's armpit.
(d) *Side by-side* (Kilian or reverse Kilian hold) upright pair spin.

Grade P8
(a) Hand-in-hand backward crossovers.
(b) Shadow three jumps, followed by controlled back outside edge (upright spiral).
(c) *Simple Loop Lift with side-by-side take off.*
(d) Combination movement – Pivot/Spiral. Man pivots, lady on back parallel spiral.

Grade P9
(a) Forward outside parallel spiral (Kilian or Reverse Kilian hold).
(b) *Shadow Salchow jump,* followed by forward outside spiral.
(c) Crossover assisted jump.
(d) Upright pair spin, meeting in waltz hold.

TEST HINTS

Grade 1. Toe pushing should be avoided. The Stop movement should be approached at a reasonable speed and must be quite positive. The two movements may be combined.

Grade 2. On the backward skating, the free foot must distinctly leave the ice.

Grade 3. The standard of the forward skating should be between the strokes required in Grade 2 and the one-third circle length required in Grade 5.

The two forward glide movements may be combined by the use of suitable linking steps.

Grade 4. The two backward glide movements may be combined by the use of suitable linking steps.

The backward to foward steps should be executed in a controlled smooth manner with neat footwork.

Grade 5. In the forward crossovers, the free foot should pass in front of the skating foot and some impetus should be gained from the outside edge of the skating foot as it leaves the ice. A smooth even movement is required. Stepping one foot over the other, tucking in, scratching from the two points and double tracking should be avoided.

Grade 6. In the backward crossovers, the free foot should pass in front of the skating foot and some impetus should be gained from the outside edge of the skating foot as it leaves the ice. A smooth even movement is required and double tracking should be avoided.

On the consecutive backward outside edges, double tracking should be avoided.

The change of edge movements (Rfo change Rfi and Lfo change Lfi) shall be skated separately, but should preferably not be started from rest. The edges should be of moderate length. The changes should be performed in the field and the arms and free leg should be used to assist the movement.

The candidates may perform outside or inside, open or closed Mohawks. The edges before and after the turns should be of approximately equal length and a reasonable degree of control is required.

Grade D7   (a) Simple Foxtrot timing is required.
           (b) As the Preliminary Test, Foxtrot Movement.

	(c) As lady's 14-Step Mohawk, also required on the other foot.
	(d) As Waltz. The three turn is turned on count 'three' and the Bo edge struck on count 'one'. The two movements may be continued with suitable linking steps.
Grade D8	(a) Simple Foxtrot timing.
	(b) As lady's Foxtrot Mohawk, also required on the other foot.
	(c) The free foot should be placed on the ice along the inner edge side of the skating foot. Following the weight transference, the positionof the new free foot is behind the heel of the skating foot. This movement should not be performed as a definite Swing Choctaw, but a degree of freedom of execution is permissible.
Grade D9	(a) Equivalent to the Preliminary Foxtrot movement performed on backward steps.
	(b) As the Blues Choctaw, also required on the other foot.
	(c) The step sequence forms a simple curve and may be repeated to form a circle.
Grade F9	(a) A substantially complete turn from Bo to Bo is required.
	(b) A degree of latitude is permissible so long as the first few rotations are definitely on the flat of the skate and the exit and entry movements are properly performed.
	(c) This sequence is serpentine (S) shaped.
Grade P7	(a) The clockwise and counter-clockwise movements should not be linked. It may be advantageous for the couple to change sides. Skating in unison while holding at arms length should be the aim.
	(b) The spiral may be skated directly on the edge following the hop, or there may be a single change of foot. Body and leg positions should be reasonably matched.
	(c) The man steps from backwards to forwards as the lady lands the jump backwards. A fully extended arm lift position is not expected at this standard.
	(d) The method of striking into the spin and free foot positions are optional, but a reasonably sustained spin of not less than three turns is required.
Grade P8	(a) Skating smoothly and in unison while holding at arm's length should be the aim.
	(b) The skaters may, if they wish, link hands on the upright spiral.
	(c) The skaters should be in the correct position at the take off for this lift (close together on back outside edges).

During the lift, the lady's hand should be firmly on the man's shoulder assisting in the lift. Provided that the positions are good, a reasonable lift, without necessarily a full extension of the man's lifting arm, is acceptable.

(d) The lady should be on a back parallel spiral with the man on a back pivot holding the lady by one hand at arm's length.

Grade P9 (a) Body and leg positions should be reasonably matched.

(b) The skaters may, if they wish, join hands on the forward spiral.

(c) Some positive lift through the hands and arms should be given, but at this standard, a lift position is not expected.

(d) The method of striking into the spin and the free foot position are optional, but a reasonably sustained spin of not less than three rotations is required.

A Note to Parents

Parents who have read this book should beware of the terrible label of 'skating parent' bestowed on certain individuals by professional coaches, judges and rink managements. Please do not interfere in any way with the coaching of your youngster, do not dispute the judges' decisions and do not criticize other skaters, trainers or competitors. You will only inculcate a prejudice against your own youngster. In other words: encourage, pay up and keep quiet!

It is generally the non-skating parent who is at fault, so, if you don't skate, get your boots and skates on and have a go! At least you'll be able to appreciate your youngster's problems . . . and you'll stop pushing him or her.

Appendix 1

Off-Ice Exercises and Fitness

In addition to learning skating skills and steps it is necessary for the enthusiastic skater to do a certain amount of exercising off the ice. These fall into the following main groups:

> Warming-up exercises
> Flexibility exercises
> Cooling-down exercises.

Skating is not just a matter of thrusting oneself along upon a blade, but involves all parts of the body. Head and neck, shoulders, arms, legs, feet, all have to play their part.

Skating, too, demands a certain amount of physical fitness even though it may be enjoyed by all ages from toddlers to senior citizens of 70 years age and older. Exercise is an activity that *stresses* a particular or specific part of the body. For example, suppose you just amble along walking — that wouldn't rate as exercise. Buf if, on the other hand, you really walked hard and fast for a few minutes, that would count as exercise. Exercise is something you have to be aware of and is focussed upon a *specific* activity or movement. Of all forms of exercise, the most important is the exercise to build up and strengthen the ability of your lungs to take in oxygen and pass it to and through the heart to the blood vessels which carry it through your body. There is a long name for this — it is called 'cardiovascular fitness'. If you just don't have this special fitness you will soon become tired and exhausted by any form of physical activity. Because cigarette smoking affects this fitness it is advisable not to start smoking, and if you already smoke, use your will power and give it up altogether.

It follows, therefore, that this is the first form of exercise you should concentrate upon. Even the simplest of ice dances can become very exhausting after a couple of circuits of the rink if your lungs are not very efficient.

MUSCLE FITNESS

This consists of muscle strength and muscle endurance. Your muscle strength is the power you have to carry out a movement. Muscle endurance is the ability to repeat this movement over and over again without getting tired. Skating ranks high in the fitness table for muscular endurance and strength, and very high in stamina. Flexibility is the way in which it is possible, using your muscles, to move various parts of yourself in different motions.

HOW TO EXERCISE

There are a number of excuses offered by people against exercise. Usually there is a first flush of enthusiasm to start exercising, and then, gradually, the exerciser becomes bored. Another, old fashioned, misconception is that exercise should be painful. Exercise, properly carried out, can be full of fun, neither boring nor painful. Exercise, under proper supervision, or under good self discipline, should not be tiring. Devoting just a few minutes a week to exercise will not make one fit.

Some people think that once one starts exercising and getting really fit, one will eat more, and build up body weight. Good exercise burns off excess calories quickly.

Naturally, young, fit people will find exercise different from more mature people. Above all, physical stature is very important in determining how exercises should be carried out.

People with well built, athletic type bodies are ideally suited for sport, fitness, and exercise of all kinds. People with slender physiques are not suited for exercises which need a lot of physical strength or weight; they are better suited for activities where skill is most important, such as climbing, long distance running, skating. Another class of person, those with soft well rounded bodies who have a tendency to be overweight, have a limited activity choice. Certainly strenuous sports and exercise are not for them, and the more physical contact sports and games should not be selected.

Manual and physical workers naturally get more exercise from their jobs than those in sedentary occupations. In fact the normal routine sitting position of the clerical worker can result in postural faults. Round shoulders or back, flat chests and paunchy tendencies of the stomach are also accompanied by slackness of thigh and buttock muscles. The office worker has to make greater use of leisure time in physical exercise to combat these tendencies than the manual worker.

Exercise necessities vary between women and men. Women and girls wish to keep their bodies supple, yet have firm muscles, and the ability to move gracefully, and with a good posture. Men and boys, on the other hand, are seekers of greater strength with flexibility. Occupations which involve physical work though keeping the worker fitter than his office counterpart may produce strong arms, and then find that the legs are not fully developed. Though he will be fitter than the clerk, he will need a certain amount of exercise to keep new muscles in trim.

Age is important. As one gets older, joints stiffen and muscles lose flexibility. The older person can still carry out exercising and it is important to do so to maintain the same weight and to stay in good condition.

No matter how well you may be skating, skating alone is not sufficient to keep you in top physical fitness. The exercises in this Appendix are to enable you to obtain strength and maintain flexibility and make your choice of activity easier. In any event, one may join a group for exercise, or carry it out under the supervision of a coach, or by oneself using a strong self discipline (which skaters need anyway). It is a sound idea for keen skaters, especially if taking it up in more mature years, to take a course or courses in Yoga. It has the great advantage that not only does it improve your body, but relaxes and refreshes the mind. This is very important for the skater wishing to take proficiency tests at a higher stage, or to enter into competitive skating.

WARMING-UP EXERCISES

Sometimes this is called 'loosening up' exercise, but it is a poor name as the joints are not made looser. These exercises make the muscles and joints used to undergoing greater movements than usual.

The exercise programme must be developed slowly and carefully and not suddenly entered into and carried out for unduly long periods. There are two main functions of warming-up exercise. In the first place it increases the circulation flow of the blood around the body, and secondly it makes the body more adaptive to the use of excessive movements, compared with normal movements. Warming-up movements do not, in fact, increase the body temperature, though there will be a slight increase in muscle temperature. What is important, however, is the psychological effect warming up has on the competitor in an athletic event.

When doing warming-up exercises, which are necessary before you do your main exercises, and which should be undertaken before getting on to the ice for a warm-up skating session prior to training or a competition, do not strain yourself, but keep to the basic number of repetitions for each exercise.

PRELIMINARY EXERCISES

These can be carried out without any special apparatus or equipment.

BREATHING

Stand in a relaxed posture, with your feet slightly apart and your arms at your sides. Take a deep breath. Exhale. Then take in a good deep breath and hold it. You should be able to hold it for at lease 40 seconds comfortably. Repeat 3 – 4 times.

FOUR EXERCISES FOR ENDURANCE

1. Stand erect with your feet together and arms down your sides. Raise your arms in line with your shoulders to each side and at the same time jump to a spread eagle position, with feet pointing forward, then jump to bring your feet together and your arms down your sides. Repeat this up to 25 times in about half-a-minute.

2. This exercise brings exercise to your knees. Stand erect then jump up and down on your toes 20 times. Try to start counting the jump (this is useful when you come to start counting ice dancing steps) one, two, three. Let your knees get well bent between each jump. You should jump off the floor about 6 inches each time.

3. Stand on your toes with your arms extended in front, with your back against a wall. Bend your knees slowly so that you achieve a squatting position, at the same time keeping your back against the wall. Then straighten your legs to return to your first position. This exercise should be carried out 10 times.

4. Lie flat on your back with your feet together and underneath something solid and which cannot be moved, such as a bed. With your arms raised in front of you slowly sit up. Do not bend the legs. Then slowly return to flat on the floor position. You should be able to do this 10 times.

Do not attempt the warm-up exercises until you are able to do these first 4 exercises easily.

RUNNING ON THE SPOT

Stand with your feet together and your arms to your side. Commence running on the spot and at the same time describe circles with your arms. Repeat 25 to 30 times. Throughout this exercise keep your head up, your shoulders back, and maintain a straight back.

LEG SWING

Stand next to a chair, or even the rink barrier, rest one hand on the chair and put the other arm out at shoulder height. Keep your head up and your back straight. If you are holding on to the chair or barrier with your left hand swing your right leg backwards and forwards 20 times. Get your leg, which should be straight, as high as you can. Then turn round, change hands, and repeat the exercise. An alternative method is to lean forward when you swing the leg backwards.

THROUGH LEG SWING

Stand with your feet apart and stretch your arms over your head. Bend your knees and slowly swing your arms between your legs and as far back as you can. Keep the arms straight. Return to the upright position and repeat 24 times.

REACH FOR THE SUN

The following exercises will enable you to build up muscle strength, flexibility, and stamina and should be carried out daily for about 30 minutes in total time. Stand with your feet parallel and apart. Raise your hands over your head and stretch upward, first with the right arm and then with the left arm as if reaching for the sun. (This is a popular Yoga exercise, too). You must feel that the entire torso is stretching. Keep your back straight throughout. Stretch for a minimum of five times with the right arm, and five times with the left. You must hold each stretch for a minimum count of 10 on each side.

BODY TWIST

Again standing with your feet parallel and apart. Hold your arms out to the sides at shoulder height. Twist your upper torso to one side and keep your feet parallel. Repeat to the opposite side. The exercise must be done slowly about 10 to 12 times each side.

SIT SPIN EXERCISE

Stand on one leg with the other stretched full length in front. Gradually bend your knee as far as possible keeping the other leg straight out in front of you with the toe pointed. Slowly move up again. Repeat on the other leg. Repeat the whole exercise several times. This exercise will help you so do a proper sit-spin, not just a spin on a half-bent knee which seems to be a sloppiness creeping into some free skaters' programmes.

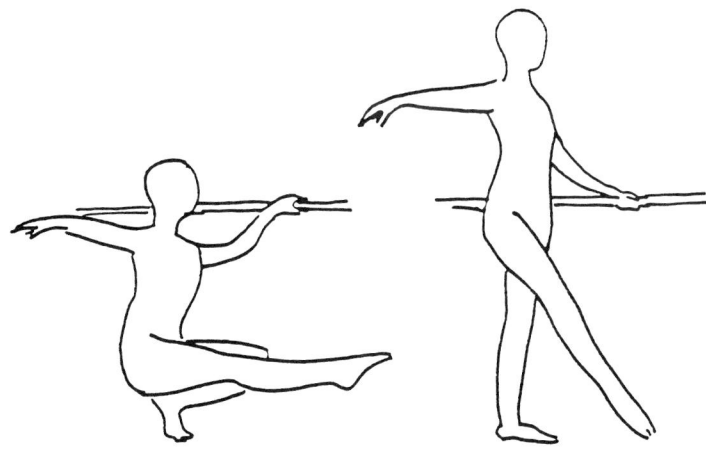

The Sit Spin Exercise

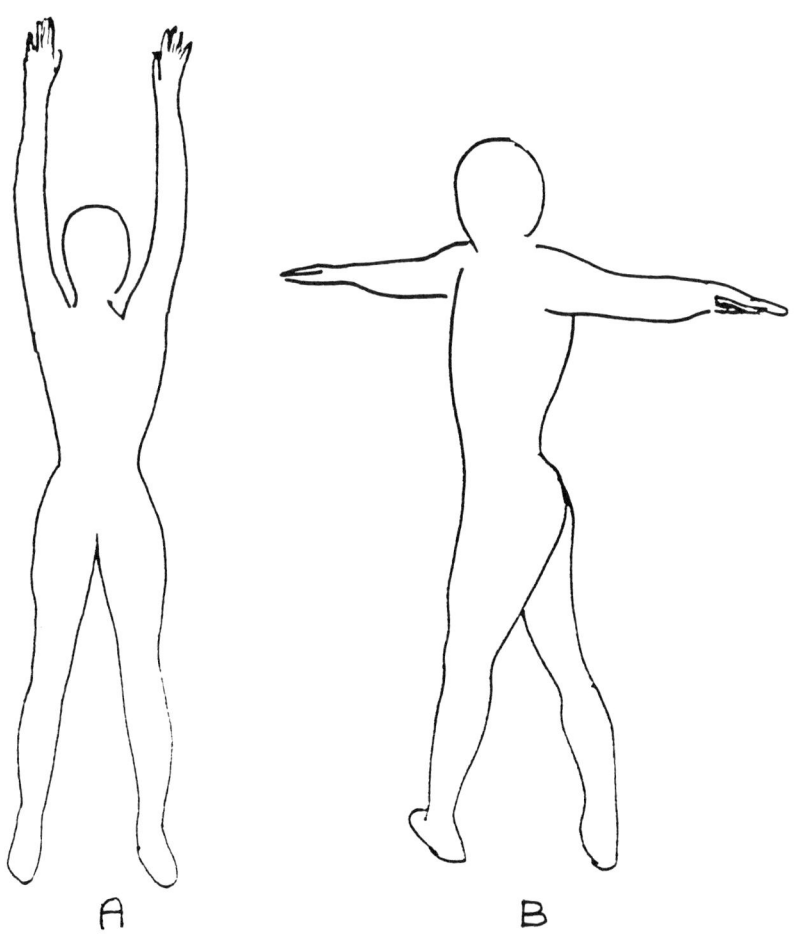

A — Reach For The Sun
B — Body Twist

THE LEG STRETCH

Lie on the floor with your arms along your sides. Raise one leg straight up with the foot flexed. Take hold of the leg behind the thigh from the opposite arm, and behind and below the calf from the arm on the side of the raised leg. Keep the leg straight and pull it down towards your chest. Release the hold and slowly lower the leg to its original position. Repeat with the other leg. The whole exercise should be repeated several times.

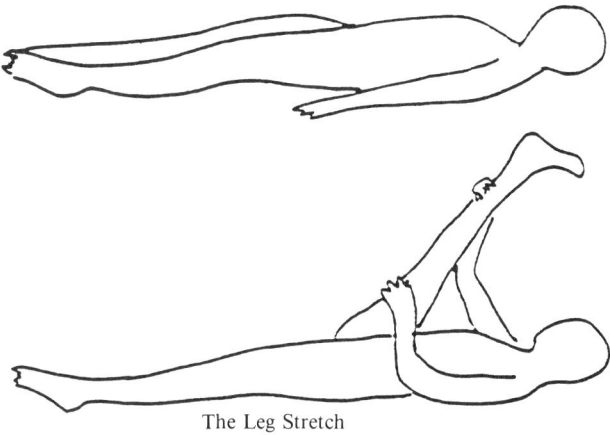

The Leg Stretch

CALF STRETCH

Stand about a yard away from a wall. Put the palms of your hands flat against the wall, then bend your elbows and lean forward. Keep your legs straight and your heels on the floor. Keep the back straight. Now press down on your heels into the floor. Hold this position for a half-a-minute. When you are able to do so gradually increase this period to two minutes.

As an alternative method you can place one foot forward and bend the knee and at the same time keep the other leg straight. Repeat by bending the other leg alternately bringing it forward and back.

THE TRIANGLE STRETCH

Again commence in a standing position with feet parallel and as wide as possible past shoulder width without strain. The feet must remain pointing to the front. Gradually bend from the waist and sink down and at the same time turn it towards the left ankle. Do not force this. Keep the legs slightly bent at the knee. Once you have this position hold it for a minute. Rise slowly and then repeat the stretch to the other side. The whole triangle exercise should be repeated two or three times.

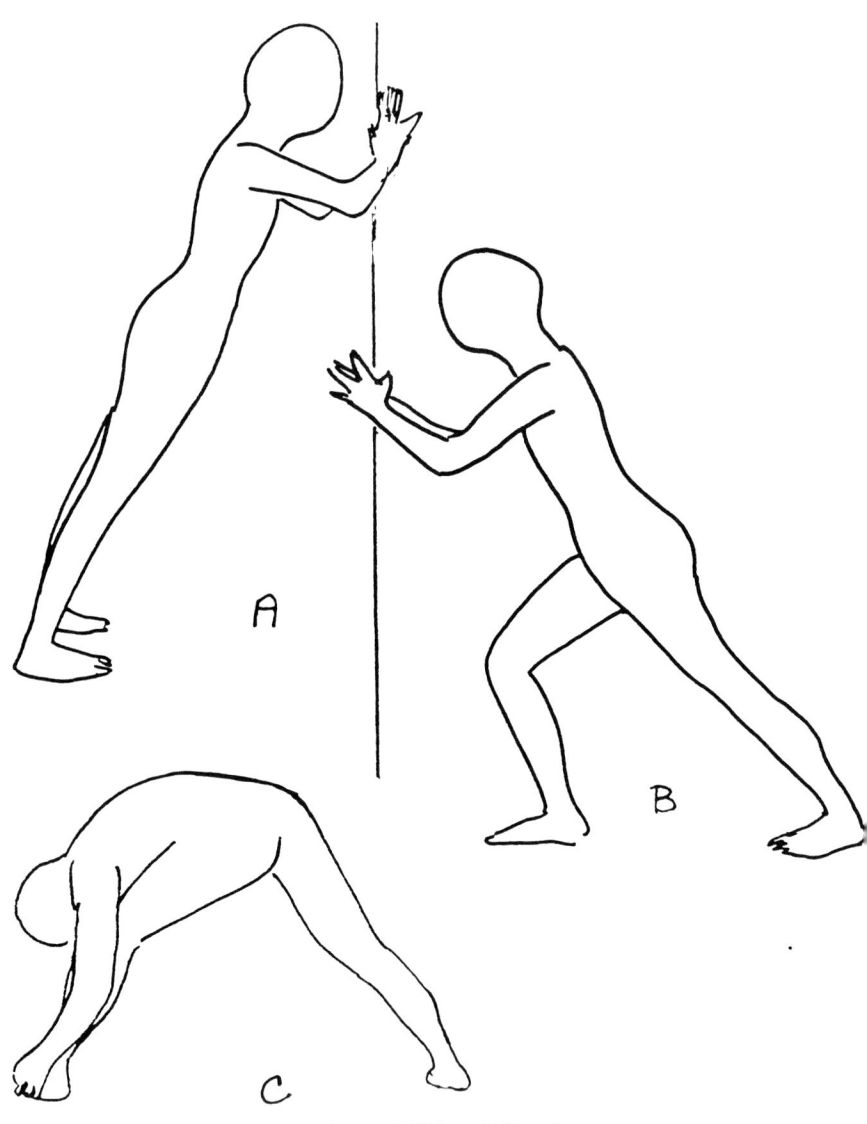

A and B — Calf Stretch Exercises
C — The Triangle Stretch

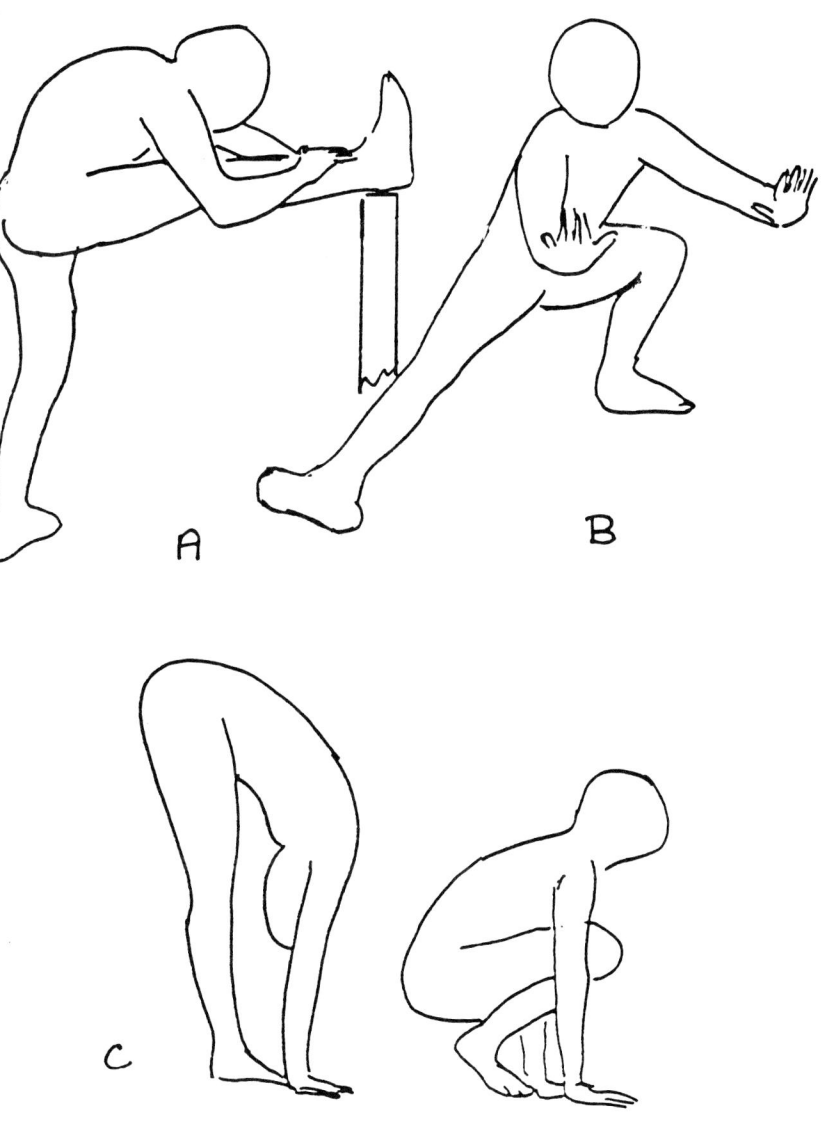

Hamstring Stretch Exercises

HAMSTRING STRETCH

There are three good hamstring exercises. In the first exercise (see drawing, A position) stand upright, lift the left leg up to waist height, higher if you can, and rest the heel on a chair back, rink barrier, or similar. Keep the leg you are standing on slightly bent at the knee. Allow your head and upper torso to come down slowly forward towards the knee of the leg which is being supported. Do not strain yourself whilst doing this. Hold this position for about 20 seconds, gradually increasing it with practice and increased flexibility to one minute. Then repeat using the other leg.

The second hamstring exercise (see drawing B position) uses a different position. First of all stand erect with your feet parallel and as wide as possible, without discomfort. Now shift your body weight to one side and bend the knee on that side very deeply. Whilst pivoting on the heel of the other foot, let yourself sink towards the floor. Hold this position for about a minute and then transfer to the opposite side, by raising and lowering the body, and hold the new position for the same length of time. The exercise should be performed a couple of times to each side. If you feel up to it, a third attempt is allowed.

The third hamstring exercise (see drawing, C position) is also particularly good for the knees. Commence the exercise in a knee-bend posture with your hands in front of you and hands flat on the floor. Bounce three or four times with your knees then straighten them. Press your heels down on to the floor and stretch your legs. Repeat this exercise several times, gradually increasing the number of repeats.

ARABESQUE

This is an important position to learn for free skating. It is a natural progression from the one leg stand which I have just described. First of all get into the one leg stand position a couple of times to get your balance right. Then when you are nice and steady in the one leg position lift one leg backwards and as high as you can without putting a lot of strain on yourself. The leg which is swung back must have the knee turned out, away from the body, and the toe nicely pointed and in line with the leg. The body is then leaned forwards with the back slightly curved upwards: ideally the foot and the head should be level. Straighten the leg you are balancing on and hold the posture nice and steady for at least one minute, two if possible.

THE PLOUGH

This is a useful exercise which stretches the muscles of the back and is also useful to help you relax.

Lie down on the floor on your back. Stretch your arms beyond your head, palms upward. Raise your legs and bottom half of your body and bring the legs forward so that the knees are beside your ears. Stay in this position for 40 to 60 seconds (when you get used to it you can stay in this position for a couple of minutes or more). Whilst in this position straighten the legs and let your toes touch the floor beyond your head. This position should also be held for the same length of time as the first half of the exercise.

SIT AND TWIST

This is another twisting exercise and is to make the muscles in the back stronger. Sit on the floor with your legs spread as far apart as is possible without feeling strain. Put your left hand on the outside of your right knee and your right hand on the floor about a foot behind your back. Slowly turn your head, upper torso, and lower part of your back, to the left as far as possible without strain. Hold this for a full minute then rotate to the other side, changing hand positions. This exercise should be repeated two or three times to each side.

ANKLE STRENGTHENING

Ankles feel the strain more than any other part of you when ice skating. These two exercise will help to strengthen them and improve the blood circulation in your feet.

Exercise one — may be done in either a standing or a sitting position. Extend your right leg forward and bend it slightly at the knee. Point the toe of this foot and rotate it at the ankle. Do this in both directions, inward and outward. Rotate the ankle for 12 times then repeat the exercise with the other leg. When you have done this part of the exercise point the toes upwards and downwards 20 times.

Exercise two requires space. Stand at one end of a room and then take 4 steps forwards on tip-toe, then 4 steps on your heels, then 4 steps on the inside of your feet, and 4 steps on the outside of your feet. Then walk backwards the same way.

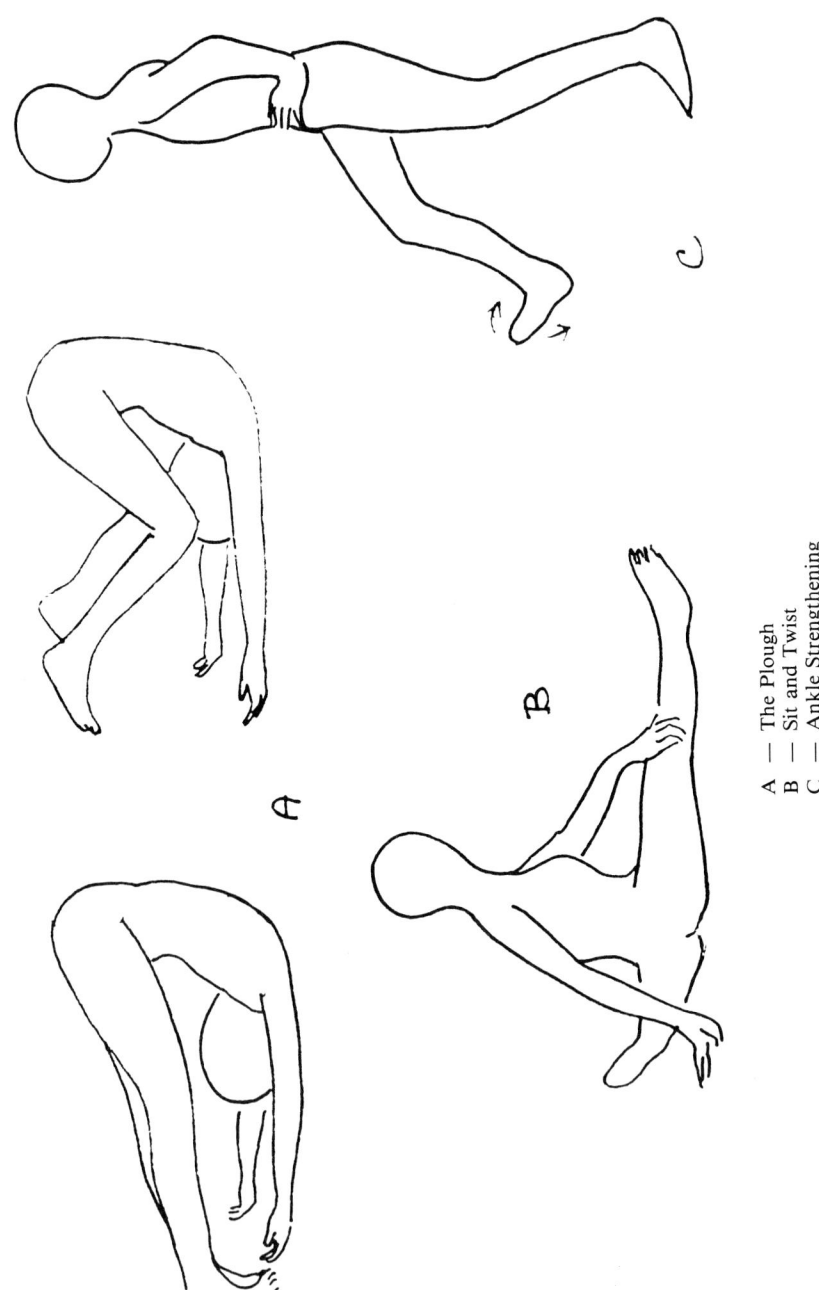

A — The Plough
B — Sit and Twist
C — Ankle Strengthening

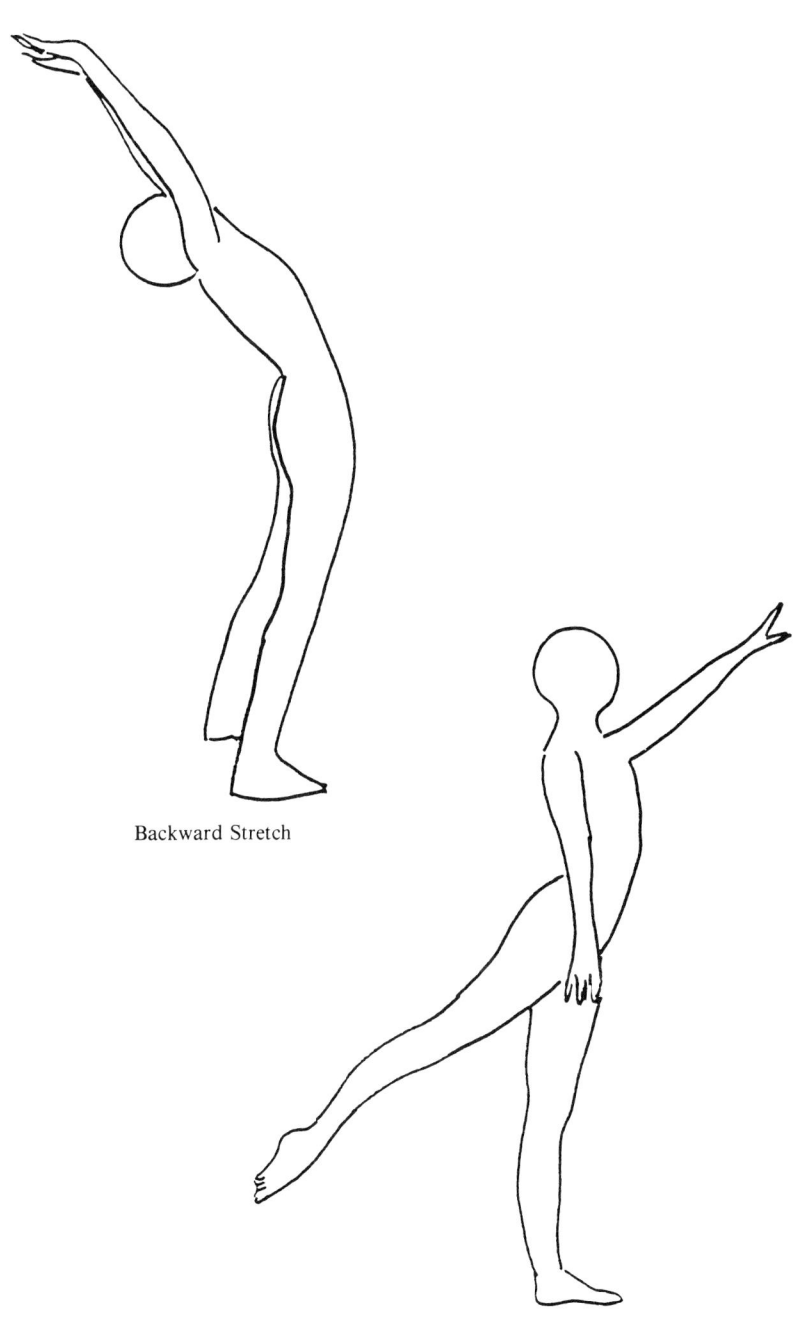

Backward Stretch

One Leg Stand

BACKWARD STRETCH

This is an exercise to strengthen the abdomen and the muscles in the lower back. Stand with your legs parallel and feet about a shoulder width apart. Raise both hands over your head and stretch upwards and over at the same time arching your back as far as is comfortable without straining. Do this for about a minute and repeat a couple of times.

ONE LEG STAND

Stand on both legs and keep the body upright. Tighten the muscles of your legs and buttocks then slide one leg backwards a few inches behind the other and point your toe. Keep the hips slightly forward. Slowly lift the backward pointing leg, which corresponds to the free leg in skating, off the floor without swinging or jerking it. Don't attempt to get your leg higher by twisting the hips. Keep your back as straight as possible and do not lean the body forward at all. Keep the body stretching upwards and your shoulders down. Hold this position steady for up to one minute. Lower the leg and then repeat on the other foot. Raise the opposite arm to the free leg, pointing forward as in the drawing, alternating with change of leg position.

SPREAD EAGLE EXERCISE

With or without skates this is a useful exercise. Stand in front of the skating barrier, or bar on a gym or dance room wall, and hold it with both hands. Your legs should be slightly apart with the feet turned out into the spread eagle position. Press your heels against the wall. Lean on to the outside edge of your skates if wearing them. Now lean backwards and push your hips forward and at the same time make certain that your knees are not bending. Hold the position for 15 seconds. Return to an upright position, Repeat two or three times.

LAY BACK EXERCISE

Hold on to the skate barrier, or bar in a gym as described for the spread eagle exercise. Hold on with both hands and keep your feet only slightly apart, with the knees straight slowly bend backwards as far as possible without discomfort. Repeat several times.

INSIDE AND UPPER THIGH KNEEL

Kneel in an upright position and keep your body absolutely straight. Gradually let your body drop backwards until your shoulders are over and in line with your toes. Come back to the upright position and then sit on your heels. Return to the upright position. Repeat several times.

SPIRAL AND BACK MUSCLES

Kneel with your hands flat on the floor. In this position bring one leg forward, until the knee touches your forehead (see diagram, position A) then push your leg backwards into an arabesque (spiral) position. (See diagram, position B). Turn the knee of the free leg outwards and stretch the foot out. As you push the leg behind you your weight is supported by your hands and the other knee. Keep your shoulders straight and your head up. You should have a good hollow in your back. Bring the free leg down to the kneeling position again, bring the other knee up to your forehead and repeat the exercise with the other leg. Repeat the whole exercise 5 to 8 times.

STANDING BEND

This is like the old toe touching exercise. Stand with your feet apart, as wide as the shoulders. Bend over as if you were going to touch your toes, and do this very slowly. If you are able to touch the floor do not do it! Just let your arms hang loosely. Hold this position for about 15 seconds. Inhale deeply into your lower abdomen, exhale, and then inhale again. Return to the standing position very slowly.

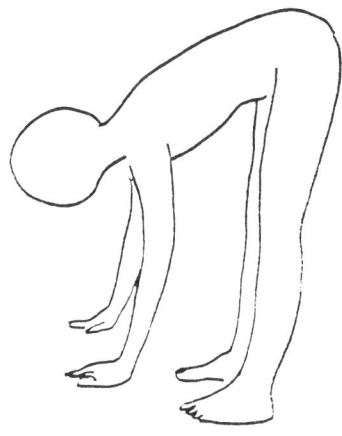

Standing Bend

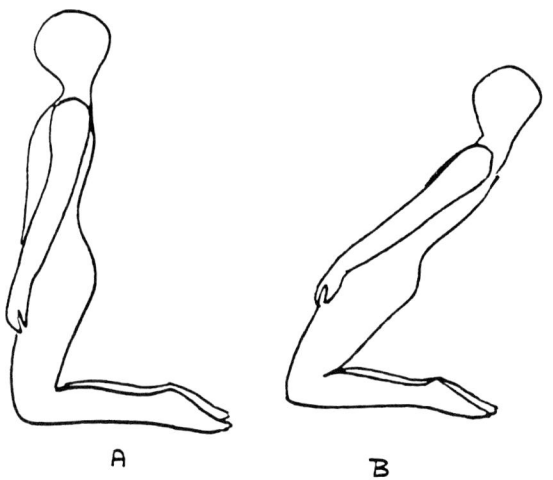

Inside and Upper Thighs Exercise

Arabesque (Spiral) and Back Strengthening Exercise

SIDE BEND

Stand with your feet well apart. Clasp your hands together behind your head. Keeping your back straight bend to one side, making sure that your elbows are well back and that your body does not lean either forwards or backwards. Return to first position and repeat to the other side. Repeat from 12 to 20 times. This has a beneficial effect on the waist, too!

SIDE BEND (VARIATION)

Stand upright with your arms down your sides with the feet apart. Keep your legs straight, and don't lean forward or backward. Bend to one side. Whilst bending slide the arm on the side you are bending, down your leg whilst the other arm slides up. Stretch and hold 5 or 6 times each side.

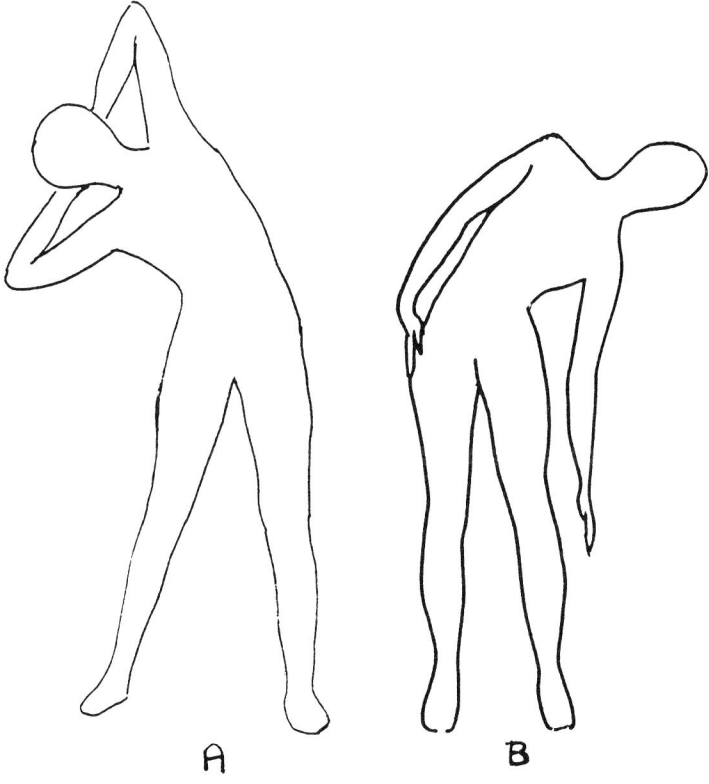

A — Side Bend
B — Side Bend Variation

WARMING-UP ON THE ICE

Good exercise is obtained by practising crossovers in both directions and concentrating on stroking. Correct stroking builds up speed easily and saves energy. Practise stroking round the rink, forwards and backwards, and extend the free leg between strokes. Do not merely saunter about the rink. Strokes may be executed in quick succession or powerfully and in slow motion. But during an official warming-up period prior to a test or competition only execute movements you are sure of: trying to attempt an unsure movement can lead to disaster, and the skater will suffer psychologically in the test or competition which immediately follows.

COOLING-DOWN EXERCISES

These are, of course, warm-ups in reverse! After a tough practice or training session, or a competition programme, it is necessary for your heart and respiration rate to come back to normal slowly. If this is not done chilling can take place, together with cramps and light-headedness. This is due to an excessive amount of blood collecting in the muscles and veins when you stop too suddenly when exercising vigorously. Cooling-down exercises allow the heart rate to slow down gradually.

Another reason for cool-down exercises is to retain the good effects you have obtained during the warming-up period and during the skating activity. So, when you have finished your training don't stop suddenly and come off the ice. Gradually slow down from vigorous skating to comfortable skating, for quite a few minutes. Of course in a championship or competition this is not always possible. Having got off the ice, and this applies to competitions and tests, shake your arms and legs, commencing with the hands and feet. Work all the way up to your shoulders and your entire legs. Then do a slowing down running on the spot, followed by reach for the sun, an ankle rotation exercise and a calf stretch.

Other Exercises

Other forms of sport and exercise can help your skating and general fitness. Cycling is especially good as it develops thigh muscles and exercises the knees. Gymnastics, modern jazz dancing, ballet are all good for you. Exercises which can be carried out to music are very helpful and modern aerobic classes, only under the supervision of trained teachers, are of value. Good, very brisk walking can help you but jogging, popular though it is, is not really good exercise for skaters.

FOOT CARE

This is very important. It is advisable to dust the inside of skating boots and socks with a good foot powder. Look after your feet and make sure that your skating boots do not cause discomfort after they have been broken in. Feet perspire after skating and they should be carefully dried before putting on your normal walking gear. This is not usually done, but a towel and foot care material in your skating bag is a wise investment. It goes without saying that toe-nails should be cut properly because an in-growing toe-nail is not only painful and should receive attention, but is the last thing you would want to happen if about to take part in a competition or skating test.

FINALLY, late nights, overtraining, alcohol, tobacco in any form, and too many fatty or sugary foods take their toll in time. You have a clear choice, so if you really want to get the best out of your chosen sport, have plenty of fun, and be fit and full of energy, pay attention to this last sentence from the first to the last letter.

Appendix II

Ice Skating Spin-Offs

It would be a very dull person who only thought of ice skating as an activity by itself. Ice skating can introduce you to many other interests, though, to be fair, they are interests relating to skating. On the other hand these interests, which I shall term, 'Ice skating spin-offs' often lead to further interests and hobbies.

These various interests or spin-offs take many forms. You may become interested in visiting other ice rinks and clubs. Some people, when taking their holidays, like to visit as many different rinks as possible, even travelling abroad for this purpose. Holiday times may become winter sporting holidays where the main interest is to skate on a rink overseas, which, in turn probably ends up with the skater also indulging in some other winter sporting activity. Visiting other rinks may be referred to as 'collecting' rinks. In turn this brings me to the first skating spin off: collecting.

COLLECTING

This may take many forms. Usually it commences when a skater visits a different rink or club and buys or is given a cloth or metal badge relating to that club or rink. Most rinks sell cloth badges which skaters sew on to their anoraks or blazers, others collect them and mount them on to a background for display on their walls at home. There are metal badges or pins as well. Once started the badge collector will find it fascinating and will find that badges can be exchanged or 'swopped' with other collectors, and that badges from overseas are in great demand.

The enthusiast may like to visit as many skating shows, amateur or professional, as possible. Along with the shows are programmes and other souvenirs which can form part of a skating collection. Programmes which carry the autographs or signature of performers will lead the collector to autograph collecting as well. The various stars at skating competitions and exhibitions become part of this special interest, and from this the collector begins to find an interest in collecting photographs of his or her favourite skater. If it can bear the star's autograph it becomes even more valuable.

Every year sees a number of foreign skaters and fans visiting British rinks. It is easy to strike up an acquaintance with them and pen friends soon became a reality. In some cases this ends up in 'swop visits', in others, where the travelling time and distances make this impossible, photographs of rinks, programmes *et cetera* can be exchanged by post.

Perhaps, with the collecting bug having bitten, the skater may wish to collect skates! Old type skates can still be found in antique and junk shops, particularly in the cheaper range of these type of shops: cleaned up they can make an interesting display or even the start of a worthwhile collection.

Another interest may lie in collecting stamps. Many countries have, in the past, celebrated winter sports and Olympic events, by depicting competitors or types of sport on their postage stamps. Skating stamps are not expensive and may well let the collector realise how interesting other branches of stamp collecting can be, perhaps becoming an avid philatelist.

Every Christmas one finds Christmas greeting cards on sale with skating scenes. Some are very artistic and well produced, generally reproductions of Dutch Old Masters with skating scenes. Some modern cards are really terrible and the skating scenes are anything but accurate and contain such things as mice or robins on skates! Nonetheless, the collector of skating greeting cards can be laying up the foundation of what could be an interesting, perhaps even valuable collection.

Further interests include skating jewellery, generally fashion jewellery, in which skates or skaters are an essential element: key rings with minature skates, tea spoons and caddy spoons with a skating motif, and pottery either with a skating scene or in figurine form.

The Christmas cards, particularly the well produced ones, may result in the collector becoming interested in art and looking for paintings and engravings which depict skating. In one National Trust property there are two marvellous bronzes, a 1925 ice figure skater, and a speed skater of the same period. When I saw these I immediately wondered just how many skaters had formed the subject of sculpture? Such a collection would be very expensive and one would need a well lined purse to fulfil it, but a collection of skating bronzes, or in wood, sounds like a wonderful one.

PHOTOGRAPHY

Apart from the collecting of photographs of notable skaters, or skating scenes, which may be obtained from retailers, photographing ones friends or relatives whilst skating can be fun and such photographs can be very important from an historical reason many years later, showing what style of skates were being used, costumes, hairstyles, and so on. Most rinks allow photography, but during national championships and competitions permission must be sought and obtained from the governing bodies running that competition. In any event, even with rink or club competitions at local level, please do not use flash photography without special permission. Flash can be distracting to a performer, and could even make a dangerous situation, especially in speed skating.

A fast film, 200 to 400 ASA film speed, with a minimum format of 35 mm film, and a good fast lens from f2, or thereabouts, with a camera capable of photographing at speeds of 1/250th to 1/500th of a second are necessary to obtain the best results. Such an interest could well lead the enthusiast into either general photography, or specialising in skating photography as a free lance for skating literature and magazines. After competitions have been decided many competitors are pleased to pose for their followers and supporters, and such pictures are more value to the photographer than those bought over the counter.

If you are interested in drawing, skaters pose a special attraction and challenge, their poses often seem to defy gravity, and armed with a pencil and sketch pad when one starts to draw skaters in action, it is surprising how much you will learn about the human body, its grace, and the actual dynamics of skating!

DRESS AND COSTUMING

To-day it is possible to buy motifs to sew on to skating dresses and outfits. Those who can knit will find that there is a challenging interest in knitting skating motifs into a jumper, giving it a personal touch which shop bought articles cannot supply. The girl, too, who can make a pleated skirt, a mini-kilt in many respects, to wear with a leotard, is on the way to making her own skating costume. Pattern houses do supply basic patterns for skating dresses, and if the result is pleasing, it can well lead to the dressmaker concerned being asked to make skating dresses for friends, club-mates, and others. Most skating dress suppliers have started off this way and do very nicely, thank you. There's an opening here for the right person.

Of course, sequins and motifs can be sewn on to skating outfits, but this can hardly be termed a hobby. The would-be dressmaker will find a wealth of modern materials in different colours and shades awaiting her — this can be a fascinating and lucrative spin-off.

BOOKS AND MAGAZINES

Skating books are eagerly sought by collectors and those which are over 100 years old are very expensive to buy. They make interesting reading and a good skating library is a fascinating aspect of the sport. There are not many worthwhile skating magazines around at the present day, but early specimens can still be obtained, chiefly through collectors and swop magazines such as *Exchange & Mart*. A current magazine, *International Skater*, to which I am a regular contributor and on the editorial staff, could well start you off on the trail of books and magazines. Perhaps a budding journalist or author will find this sort of spin-off becoming an interest leading to a professional occupation.

The club member who sends in reports to local papers and the skating journals may well find that he or she has an increasing interest in the sport, perhaps coupled with photography, and this would be a valuable interest to cultivate.

PROFESSIONAL CAREER

If you are successful in passing proficiency tests or winning competitions you may consider teaching skating as a career, or even wish to become a member of a skating show.

Skating teaching requires a good knowledge of the technical side of the sport coupled with an insight into pupil psychology. No two pupils are alike, and class work can be more confusing. A skating teacher must have knowledge of the sport, a love of teaching, a rapport with each pupil, and a keen desire to help each and every pupil achieve their desires whether it be just to circulate the rink and be able to stop, or an ambition to skate in international championships. To be a teacher you must also be a Father Confessor and confidante — you must be able to encourage, and at the same time put the brakes on when necessary, and when the moment comes when you have taught a pupil all you can, you must be ready to pass that pupil on to a specialist coach who will build on that sound basic background you have imparted.

Show skating is a different proposition. You may skate in a chorus line, or be a supporting act, perhaps even some day becoming a star. If you have been a competition skater you must remember that the audience do not understand skating technicalities. It is your job to give them a worthwhile and interesting presentation of skating movements in an artistic and interpretive manner. You must give them of your best, and you must leave them wanting more. You must have time and interest to talk to fans who visit you after a show, you must be prepared to spend a little time encouraging them, autographing their programmes, and photographs. But you will have a limited life as a show skater, after which you can become a coach or teacher, though it will give you the opportunity to travel the world.

Other professional jobs connected with skating include skate shop assistance, later management, where you will advise customers on choice of skates and costumes, etc. Perhaps you are musically inclined and have Disc Jockey ambitions: there are openings here for skaters who can present music for skaters!

Skating spin-offs are many and varied — they are there to give you joy and satisfaction long after your skating days are over — though you may well skate into pensioner years!

Glossary or Mini-Dictionary of Skating Terms

ACCENTED BEAT — The stress of one tone over others in music — the accented beat is the emphasised, or strong, beat.

ACCURACY — An essential element in ice dancing and in figure skating. In ice dancing the steps, timing, and movement of the dancers must be in accordance with the regulations.

AIM — The direction in which a starting stroke, sequence, or step is made.

ARABESQUE — A body position with the free leg extended and which is in line with the body, or curved upwards. It is skated on a sustained edge, not necessarily curved.

AXEL — short for AXEL PAULSEN: A jump from a forward outside edge on one foot with 1½ turns in the air and landing on the back outside edge of the other foot. It takes its name from the Norwegian skater, Axel Paulsen, who invented it.

AXIS — An imaginary line bisecting a rink or skating figure.
AXES, plural of AXIS.

These are: CONTINUOUS AXIS — an imaginary continuous line running around the rink surface around which a dance pattern is placed.

Usually a Continuous Axis has two straight lines along the length of the rink, approximately midway between the centre line of the rink and the barrier. The axis is connected at each end by semi-circles. However, some dances, such as the Fourteen Step are circular dances, in which case the Continuous Axis is a circle.

Other axes are LONGITUDINAL — in ice dancing this is the midline of the rink from end to end. In figure skating this is an imaginary straight line running the length of a figure and bisecting it. It is also an imaginary line around which consecutive half-circles are grouped, called the LONG AXIS.

MAJOR AXIS — another name for the LONG AXIS.

TRANSVERSE AXIS — this is an imaginary line which bisects the LONGITUDIAL AXIS at right angles or intersects the CONTINUOUS AXIS at right angles (sometimes called the SHORT AXIS).

BACKWARD INSIDE EDGE — The curve made by a skater who travels backwards with the centre of the curve inside the inside edge of the skate.

BACKWARD OUTSIDE EDGE — The curve made by a skater who is travelling backwards with the centre of the circle on the inside of the outside edge of the blade.

BAR — A measure of music which consists of a set number of beats, of which the first is accented.

BARRIER — The structure around the surface of an ice rink, usually of wood.

BEAT — The regular recurring and periodic pulse that is the unit of measurement in measured music.

BLADE — The vertical section of a metal skate, the bottom of which is ground with a hollow to form two sharp edges. Another name for skate, or boot and skate.

BRACKET — A turn made on one foot from forward to backwards or *vice versa* from an edge of one character to an edge of another character, e.g. outside edge to inside edge. The turn is made with a contra rotation against the curve of the beginning edge.

BUNNY HOP — A simple jump in which the skater travels forward without any turn, lands on the toe of the other foot and immediately on to the blade of the jumping foot.

CENTRE — The point where long and short axes intersect: this is the starting and ending point of a figure.

CHANGE OF EDGE — When skating on one foot the skater rocks over from one edge to the opposite one, e.g. from inside edge to outside edge, thus forming a SERPENTINE PATTERN or tracing on the ice.

CHASSÉ — A dance step in which the free foot is placed on the ice beside the skating foot, and the new free foot leaves the ice beside the new skating foot.

CHASSÉ MOVEMENT or **CHASSÉ SEQUENCE** — A sequence in which after the execution of a chassé, the skater strikes on to the original outside edge.
See CROSS CHASSÉ

CHERRY FLIP — See TOE LOOP JUMP.

CHOCTAW — A turn from one foot to another, from forward to backward to forward, on edges of different character, e.g. outside to inside or *vice versa*.
CLOSED CHOCTAW — Is one in which the free foot is placed on the ice along the outer edge of the skating foot, near the heel. Following the transfer of the skater's weight the new free foot is in front of the toe of the skating foot.
OPEN CHOCTAW — A choctaw in which the free foot is placed on the ice on the inner side of the skating foot. After the transfer of the skater's weight the new free foot is behind the heel of the new skating foot.
SWING CHOCTAW — Is one in which the free foot moves past the skating foot before returning to the skating foot to execute the turn. It may be open or closed choctaw.
A CHOCTAW May be CROSSED OR UNCROSSED. In a CROSSED CHOCTAW the feet are crossed either in front or behind but the tracings do not cross one another. In an UNCROSSED CHOCTAW the tracings cross but the feet do not cross.

CLOSED — A position in which the free side of the body is held towards the direction in which the toe of the skating foot is pointed.

CLOSED CHOCTAW — See CHOCTAW.

CLOSED HOLD — See WALTZ HOLD.

CLOSED MOHAWK — See MOHAWK.

COUNTER — A turn made on one foot either forward to backward or backward to forward. The turn is from one edge to an edge of the same character, e.g. inside to inside. The turn is contra to the natural direction of progress on the first edge. Edges before and after the turn are on different lobes, giving a serpentine effect.

CROSS CHASSÉ — A chassé in which the free foot is placed on the ice crossed behind the skating foot when skating forwards. When skating backwards the free foot is crossed in front of the skating foot.

CROSS OVER — A movement commenced on the outside edge of one foot, forward or backward, in which the free foot passes around and in front of the skating foot, and is placed on an inside edge.

CROSS ROLL — A sequence of movements in which the skater commences on a forward outside edge, the free foot passes around and ahead of the skating foot and the impetus for the stroke on to the outside edge of the other foot is obtained from the outside edge of the foot about to become the free foot. A serpentine tracing follows. Cross rolls may be forward or backward.

CROSS STEPS — *See* STEP.

CROSS STROKE — *See* STROKE.

DANCE — A sequence of steps performed to music by two partners, lady and man. Compulsory dances are skated to a pattern with repeats of the dance sequence to music of a specific tempo and rhythm. Free dances consist of a programme of steps and sequences using dance steps and free skating movements, of a non-repetitive nature. This must not have the character of a pair skating programme. There are restrictions on lift, spins and separating movements.
ORIGINAL SET PATTERN DANCE is one prescribed in competitions and tests to a definite rhythm and tempo to test the inventiveness and skill of the couple and the dance has to be skated to a certain number of sequences which have to be placed at the same place on the rink.

DANCE SEQUENCES — are consecutive steps which either form a complete dance or a section of it.

DANCE STEPS — in ice dancing consist of edges or parts thereof, and turns.
In Free Skating they are a sequence of edges, usually skated to music and forming a link between jumps, spins, and other movements. Sometimes called LINKING STEPS.

DEPTH OF EDGE — The extent of the curvature of the edge.

EDGE — Either of the two sharp sides of an ice blade. An edge is also the result of a skater leaning in a manner which causes one edge of the blade to bite or cut into the ice.

EIGHT — A compulsory or school figure consisting of two circles which start and finish at a centre point between them. An eight should be about three times the height of the skater in diameter of the circle. In the Preliminary Ice Figure Skating Test of the NSA three strokes are allowed before starting the figure: in all other tests the figures are commenced from rest, i.e. from a standstill.

EMPLOYED — A term used to describe the skating foot and those parts of the body and limbs on that side of the skater, e.g. skating on the left foot, the left side and arms and hip would be termed 'employed'.

EXPRESSION — Defined as the quality of ice dancing which interprets the character of the music that designates the type of dance, e.g. waltz, tango, foxtrot, polka, march etc.

EXTENDED HOLD — Also known as the HAND – IN – HAND POSITION.

FIESTA TANGO — A dance, on both ice and rollers, in which the partners skate in REVERSED KILIAN hold, both skating identical steps.

FIGURE — This refers to the officially recognised two or three-lobed geometrical designs referred to as 'SCHOOL' or COMPULSORY FIGURES, on which tests and competitions are based.

FIGURE SKATE — A type of skate used for figure skating and free skating.

FIGURE SKATING — Also known as ARTISTIC SKATING. This is a generic term covering FIGURES, or prescribed geometrical patterns traced on the ice as well as FREE SKATING, PAIR SKATING, and DANCE SKATING.

FLAT — The tracing made when a skater does not travel on either edge but on the full width of the blade.

FOOTWORK — Also known as dance steps.

FORWARD — When this term is used in connection with part of the body, it indicates that it is in front of the toe of the employed foot, or pressing directionally in the way in which the skating foot is pointing whether or not the skater is travelling forwards or backwards.

FORWARD INSIDE EDGE — The curve made when a skater travels forward leaning over so that he traces the curve with the inside edge of the skate blade.

FORWARD OUTSIDE EDGE — The curve made when a skater travels forward and leaning so that he traces the curve with the outside edge of the blade.

FOURTEEN STEP — A lively dance, skated in a set pattern, to march music.

FOXTROT MOVEMENT — An elementary dance consisting of basic forward edges only. Skated by partners in the Kilian Hold and skating the same steps to Foxtrot Tempo music.

FREE — The side and parts of the body on the opposite side to the EMPLOYED side. Thus, free foot, free shoulder etc.

FREE SKATING — A section of figure skating which consists of movements, turns, jumps, spins, spirals, dance steps and other techniques such as spread eagles, pivots as opposed to COMPULSORY FIGURE SKATING. It is skated to music in a programme to show inventiveness, technical ability and excellence of performance.

GLIDE WALTZ — A simple dance to waltz tempo, skated in Kilian Hold, consisting of forward chassé steps, with a long inside edge held round end of rink steps.

GRINDING — The process by which the two edges of the skate are kept sharp and the hollow between them restored.

HAND-IN-HAND — A dance hold in which the hand of one partner is held by one hand of the other. The arms are extended. Partners face in the same direction.

HOCKEY STOP — A method of stopping when skating in which both hips are swung to one side against the line of travel and both skates are in line with the hips.

ICE DANCING — Based on ballroom dancing on ice and executed by a male and female partner in holds recognised officially.

INSIDE EDGE — The edge of the skating blade or the tracing which it makes is to the left of the right skating foot and to the right of the left skating foot, no matter whether the skater is travelling forwards or backwards.

INTERPRETATION (MUSICAL) — This refers to ice dancing and is a combination of correct timing in all its aspects, and the individual expression which emphasises the character of the music.

KILIAN HOLD — Sometimes called Kilian Position. The partners in this dance hold face in the same direction. The man's right shoulder should be behind the lady's left. The left arm of the lady is extended in front across the man's body to his left hand. His right arm is behind her back. Both right hands are clasped and rest over the lady's hip bone at her waist. This hold is used in both ICE DANCING and PAIR SKATING.
(*See* REVERSED KILIAN).

LEAN — The inclination of the body on the skate.

LOBE — In ice dancing a lobe is the pattern which is traced on the ice by any step, or sequence of steps, which corresponds to an arc of a circle on one side of the continuous axis. In figures, lobes are the circles and half circles which make up a figure. Compulsory figures consists of two-lobed and three-lobed figures.

LONG AXIS — *See* AXIS

MAJOR AXIS — *See* AXIS.

MAJOR EDGE — The edge which carries the weight of the skater.

MEASURE — Also known as BAR in music. This is a group of beats, and all measures in a given time of music contain the same number of beats.

MELODY — This is the leading part of a harmonised musical composition. The melody line determines the phrasing of the musical composition and melody may be said to be a succession of simple sounds which are so arranged to have a pleasant effect. It may be described as the 'tune or song'. The melody is usually made up of upper range or high sounds and should be mainly disregarded by the performers with respect to proper timing in ice dancing.

MINOR AXIS *See* AXIS — short axis.

MOHAWK — A turn from one foot to the other, forward or backward or backward to forward. It has edges of the same character, thus inside to inside. The kinds of MOHAWK are:

UNCROSSED MOHAWK — A mohawk which has tracings crossing but the feet do not cross.

CROSSED MOHAWK — A turn when the feet are crossed in front or behind but the tracings do not cross each other.

CLOSED MOHAWK — Here the free foot is placed on the ice along the outer edge side of the skating foot, at the heel. After the transfer of the skater's weight the position of the new free foot is in front of the toe of the skating or employed foot. The turn gets its name from the final closed free hip position.

OPEN MOHAWK — In this the free foot is placed on the ice along the inner edge side of the skating foot. It is aimed approximately heel to instep. After the weight transfer the new free foot is behind the heel of the new skating foot. This gets its name from the final open free hip position.

SWING MOHAWK — This may be either open or closed. The free leg is swung forward past the skating foot and brought back close beside the skating foot before executing the turn.

NATURAL ROTATION — This is the natural direction of rotation by the skater's body following the curve of the edge on which he/she is skating. Thus if a skater is travelling on a forward outside edge on the left foot, this would tend to rotate the body to the left (in an anticlockwise direction).

OLYMPIC FOXTROT — A simple dance in Kilian Hold which may be skated on both ice and rollers.

OPTIONAL PATTERN — This is a dance pattern which may be skated to various patterns to suit rink conditions but still preserving the correct edges and timing

PAIR SKATING — A branch of figure skating skated by a couple, man and lady, involving free skating movements including lifts, spins, executed in unison and in harmony by both skaters.

PATTERN — In ice dancing this is the design of an ice dance which stipulates where the edges and turns of an ice dance are laid out on the ice.

PICK — *See* TOE PICK or TOE RAKE.

PIVOT — A free skating movement in which the skater places the toe rake or toe pick in the ice and circles round it. In a forward pivot the circle is made on an inside edge: in a back pivot the circle is traced by the outside edge of the circling skate. A variation may consist of the skater commencing the movement on an inside back edge and placing the toe pick on the ice whilst continuing the movement.

PROGRESSIVE — *See* RUN.

ROCKER — A turn made on one foot from forwards to backwards, or *vice versa*, and maintaining edges of the same character, e.g. inside to inside, outside to outside. The turn is made in the natural rotation of the curve being skated up to the point of turn. Edges before and after the turn have opposite directional curves.

ROCKOVER — A change of lean from one side to the other.

ROLL — An edge, usually about one-third of a circle which curves in the opposite direction to the preceding edge skated on the other foot.

RUN (also called a PROGRESSIVE) — This is a step or sequence of steps on the same curve and in the same direction in which the free foot, whilst becoming the skating foot, strikes the ice beside and travels past the skating foot. The new free foot leaves the ice and trails the new skating foot, in such a way that some impetus is obtained from the edge of the foot becoming the new free foot.

In FREE SKATING a RUN is a succession of CROSSOVERS used to get up speed prior to a jump, etc.

SALCHOW — A jump which consists of one turn in the air. The take-off is from a back inside edge on one foot to a back outside edge of the other. It gets its name from former world champion Ulrich Salchow who invented it.

SNOW PLOUGH — A method of stopping or reducing speed. It is a two footed movement in which both toes are turned inwards thereby causing the blades to skid, and bring the skater to a stop.

SPIRAL — An arabesque (*see*) on a curved edge which decreased in radius.

SPREAD EAGLE — A skating position in which both feet are turned out with the legs extended, and travelling in line leading with the toe of one foot and the trailing with the toe of the other.

STEP — This is defined as the visible tracing on the ice of a one footed movement, unless otherwise specified. A step consists of edges or parts of edges and turns, for example, three and rockers etc.

SEQUENCES OF STEPS in ice dances consist of consecutive steps from which a dance sequence is made up.

STEPS consist of OPEN STROKES, CROSS STROKES, CROSSED STEPS FORWARD AND BEHIND.

OPEN STROKE — this is commenced close beside the skating foot and not crossed either forward or behind.

CROSS STROKE this is a step started with the feet crossed. The impetus is obtained from the outside edge of the foot which is becoming the free foot.

CROSSED STEPS FORWARD occur when the free foot is placed on the ice along the outer edge of the skating foot. The calf of the crossing leg being crossed in front of the shin of the skating leg.

CROSSED STEPS BEHIND occur when the free foot is placed on the ice along the outer edge side of the skating foot, the shin of the free leg being crossed behind the calf of the skating leg.

TEMPO — The speed of the music used in ice dancing by measures per minute, and the number of beats per measure: beats per minute.

THREE JUMP (also termed WALTZ jump) — A jump in which the skater takes off from a forward outside edge on one foot, makes a half turn in the air, and lands on a back outside edge of the other foot.

THREE TURN — A turn made on one foot, with a natural rotation along the curve prior to the turn, from an edge of one character to an edge of a different character: e.g. outside forward to inside back. The turn may be made from forwards to backwards or *vice versa*.

TIMING (in ICE DANCING) — The correct relationship of the stroke and glide of the skate on the ice, with other body movements, to the correct beats of the music.

TOE LOOP JUMP (or CHERRY FLIP) — A jump in which the skater is assisted by the toe pick on the ice.

The skater takes-off from a back outside edge, strikes the ice with the toe pick of the free foot, and makes one turn in the air, landing on the original back outside edge.

TOE PICK — The serrated projections at the front of an ice figure or dance skate used to grip the ice in certain spins and jumps. Also termed a 'toe rake' or 'tooth'.

TRACING — The white mark left on the ice made by the blade of the skate.

T – STOP — A stop in which the free foot is placed on the ice behind the skating foot and at right angles to it. The pressure of the trailing foot on the ice brings the skater to a stop. Also the starting position prior to first stroke.

WALTZ POSITION — A position in ice dancing in which the lady and man face each other. The man's left arm is extended to the left and his left hand holds the lady's right hand. Her left hand rests on his right upper arm, elbow resting on elbow. The man's right hand is under her shoulder on her back. A ballroom dancing position.

Index

Arabesque .... 70,71,87,87, Glossary
Axel Paulsen jump .... 96, Glossary
Axis, Axes .... 20,21,33,34, Glossary

Back inside eight .... 39 – 46
Back outside eight .... 38 – 39
Backward Crossover 31
Backward skating 22,23,24,25
    stopping 25
Body positions 35,36,37,39,40
Boots, lacing of 4,5
    requirements of 5,6
    sizes of, British & Continental 6
Bracket turn .... 45,46 Glossary
Bunny Hop Jump .... 72,73, Glossary

Changes of edge 40,41,42,43
    forward .... 41 – 42
    backwards 42,43
Chassé .... 29,30,27 – 29, Glossary
    crossed 29,30
    open .... 27 – 29
Cherry Flip Jump
    see TOE LOOP JUMP
Choctaw .... 48, Glossary
Circle Eights .... 35 – 44
Clothing 2,3,4, 93
Clubs 94
Competitions .... 85 – 86
Compulsory Figures 17,20
Counter .... 45,47, Glossary
Crossed Chassé
    see CHASSÉ
Cross-overs 15,16,31
Curves 21

Dance Holds 53,54,55,56,57,59,60,
    .... 61 – 63,66
Dance Skates 8
Dance Skating ..... 27 – 34,52 – 69,78,80
    choosing partner for 52
    comparison with ballroom 32
Dance Steps, Freeskating 78,80
Death Spiral 87,90
Drag 80,81

Edges 13,14,15
    see also CHANGES OF EDGE
    of skate 13
Elementary Grade Tests 73,74,76,99 – 108
European Waltz .... 63 – 65
    Faults in 64
    Pattern off 63,64
    Steps .... 63 – 65

Falling 13
Feet, care of 4
Fiesta Tango 54,68,69
    Pattern of 69
    Steps .... 68 – 69
Figure skates 8,17
Figure Skating, positions of body 19
    terms 18
First steps 9,10
Form, good, rules for 17,18
Forward Inside Eight 38
    Outside Eight 35,36
Fourteen Step .... 65 – 67
    Pattern for 67
    Steps 66,67
Foxtrot Hold 53,55
Foxtrot Movement ...... 58,59, Glossary
    Pattern 58
    Steps 58,59
Free Skating .... 17,70 – 91
    Programmes for .... 82 – 86
    Skates for 8

Glide Waltz .... 56,57, Glossary

Hand-in-Hand Hold 53
Hockey Stop 11,12
Hollow Grinding of Skate 13

Inside Edge of Skate 13
Inside Forward Curves 22
International Style 17

Jumps and Jumping .... 71 – 79

147

Kilian Hold 54,55,58,88
Knee Action 15,16,33

Mohawk .... 47 – 51, Glossary
Music 32,33

National Skating Association 27,56,58,62,
.... 73,74,98,100

Olympic Foxtrot ..... 60,61,62, Glossary
   Pattern of 61
   Steps .... 60 – 62
One Footed Turns .... 45 – 47
Open Chassé
   see CHASSÉ
Outside Edge, of skate 13
Outside Forward Curves 21
Outdoor Skating .... 92 – 93
   Dangers of 93

Pair Lifts .... 90 – 91
   Spins 89
   Skating .... 86 – 91
      Finding a Partner for ..... 86 – 87
      Unison important 86
Patterns in Dancing 32,33
Pirouettes
   see SPINS
Pivots .... 84,85, Glossary
Preferred Pattern 32
Preliminary Foxtrot
   see FOXTROT MOVEMENT
Preliminary Tests 21
Preliminary Waltz
   see WALTZ MOVEMENT
Professional Coaching 94
Proficiency Tests
   see TESTS
Progressives
   see RUN
Programmes (Free Skating) 82,86

Reversed Kilian Hold 54,55
Rink, choice of 1
   discipline 1,2
Rolls 21
Rocker .... 45,46, Glossary
Run 30,31

Salchow Jump 76,77
School Figures 17
   see also COMPULSORY FIGURES
Set Pattern 32
Shadow Skating 88
Skate Guards 5
Skates, hiring of 4
   types of 7,8,13,14
Snow Plough Stop 11,12
Spins 78
Spirals 70,71,87
Spread Eagle 80,81,82
Stopping when skating 11,12
Stroke, skating 10,11,15

T-position ... 10,11,13,15,21,22,32,49,50
T-stop 12
Tango, Fiesta .... 68 – 69
   Hold 54,55
Teapot 80,81,83
Tempo of music 32
Tests .... 94,95,98 – 108
Three Jump 73,74,77
Three Turn 45,46,49,50
Toe Loop Jump .... 74 – 76,77
Toe Picks 14
Turns .... 25,26,45 – 51
Two Footed Jump 83
Two Footed Turns .... 47 – 51

Waltz, European .... 63 – 65
   Hold 53
   Jump
      see THREE JUMP
   Movement 62,63
Warming-Up Periods 85,86
Weight Transfer 15,16

148